Empathy and Performance

PERFORMING LATIN AMERICAN & CARIBBEAN IDENTITIES

Performing Latin American and Caribbean Identities

KATHRYN BISHOP-SANCHEZ, *series editor*

This series is a forum for scholarship that recognizes the critical role of performance in social, cultural, and political life. Geographically focused on the Caribbean and Latin America (including Latinidad in the United States) but wide-ranging in thematic scope, the series highlights how understandings of desire, gender, sexuality, race, the postcolonial, human rights, and citizenship, among other issues, have been explored and continue to evolve. Books in the series will examine performances by a variety of actors with under-represented and marginalized peoples getting particular (though not exclusive) focus. Studies of spectators or audiences are equally welcome as those of actors—whether literally performers or others whose behaviors can be interpreted that way. In order to create a rich dialogue, the series will include a variety of disciplinary approaches and methods as well as studies of diverse media, genres, and time periods.

Performing Latin American and Caribbean Identities is designed to appeal to scholars and students of these geographic regions who recognize that through the lens of performance (or what may alternatively be described as spectacle, ceremony, or collective ritual, among other descriptors) we can better understand pressing societal issues.

Other titles in the series:

Empathy and Performance

Enactments of Power in Latinx America

LAURA V. SÁNDEZ

Vanderbilt University Press
Nashville, Tennessee

Library of Congress Cataloging-in-Publication Data

Names: Sández, Laura V., author.
Title: Empathy and performance : enactments of power in Latinx America /
    Laura V. Sández.
Description: Nashville, Tennessee : Vanderbilt University Press, [2024] |
    Series: Performing Latin American and Caribbean identities ; 6 |
    Includes bibliographical references.
Identifiers: LCCN 2024011404 (print) | LCCN 2024011405 (ebook) | ISBN
    9780826506740 (hardcover) | ISBN 9780826506733 (paperback) | ISBN
    9780826506757 (epub) | ISBN 9780826506764 (pdf)
Subjects: LCSH: Performing arts--Psychological aspects. | Performing
    arts--Audiences--Psychology. | Empathy. | Power (Psychology) | Hispanic
    American actors.
Classification: LCC PN1590.P76 S26 2024 (print) | LCC PN1590.P76 (ebook)
    | DDC 792.089/68073--dc23/eng/20240530
LC record available at https://lccn.loc.gov/2024011404
LC ebook record available at https://lccn.loc.gov/2024011405

Front cover image: Josefina Baez, *Dominicanish*.
Photo by Luisa Sanchez for Ay Ombe Theatre, 2002.

For Neil, my friends, and family

I must be the bridge to nowhere
But my true Self
And then
I will be useful.
　　　　　—RUSHIN "THE BRIDGE POEM"

Verbal art may comprehend both myth narration
and the speech expected of certain members of
society whenever they open their mouths, and it is
performance that brings them together in culture-
specific and variable ways.

　　　　　—BAUMAN, *VERBAL ART AS PERFORMANCE*

CONTENTS

ILLUSTRATIONS

ACKNOWLEDGMENTS

I WOULD LIKE to give thanks for the support of those who made it possible for me to be in a position to write and publish this work.

First of all, to Neil, my partner in life, who has been hearing about this project since its beginnings, and whose feedback I benefited from.

I am grateful for the extensive time that Nao Bustamante, Josefina Báez, Alex Torra, Kukuli Velarde, and Levi Rickert generously shared with me. I am also grateful for the role they play in the art world and/or in society at large.

A special thanks to community members, co-workers, students, and professors whose direct and indirect support propelled me forward in crucial times, among them, Nancy and C., Chris B., Tania, Chris P., and Molly from the Timberline group; Elizabeth Williamson and David Wolach at TESC, who first told me about a field of study called "performance studies" back in 2007; Roger Smith and Linda Austin in PDX; Rafa at NYU; and Licia Fiol-Matta, at the Graduate Center and then at NYU.

Last but not least, thanks to the editorial team at VUP, to all those who made the logistics of this book possible. And to Zack, for believing in this book project from the start.

Introduction

THIS BOOK IS about empathy and enactments of power in performances that reflect on experiences of otherness in the United States. It studies the dramatized dilemma of cultural understanding in Latinx America, "our America" in the US. This notion that encompasses self and other, in-group and out-group relations, refers first to a collective political identity marking a common belonging in the Spanish speaking America, but at the same time, alludes to current struggles in the contemporary USA. Some readers might be familiar with José Martí's essay "Our America," which borrowed from newly established narratives of self-representation around the notion of Latin America.[1] As a political identity, it never had a fixed meaning, but this 'belonging' grew from some foundational antinomies: European vs. American; imperialism vs. anti-imperialism; colonialism vs. anti-colonialism, that later subdivided the American continent in "two Americas."[2] The diverse Latinx population living in the United States today has further complicated this division.[3] Nowadays, what defines a unique otherness is continuously shifting, and more than one kinship option is often embraced. Yet, prevalent notions of self and other, in-group and out-group relations continue relating to the imperial and colonial legacies that informed Martí's essay. The focus of this study is the concept of empathy at the boundaries of two kinship positions.[4]

Otherness from the perspective of the dominant is often simplified to mean "what-is-not," but for different minoritarian groups, the ways of performing identity and otherness are not monolithic.

Conceptualizing empathy requires understanding how subjects organize, classify, and limit themselves, not only as agents but also as interpreters. What sorts of affiliations do these performances promote? How do they break, reinforce, or queer societal expectations about the Latinx body, the white body, or simply the staged body? To survey different answers to these queries, *Empathy and Performance* examines an array of artistic enactments, produced between 1992 and 2021: *Indigurrito* (Nao Bustamante), *Dominicanish* (Josefina Báez), *¡Bienvenidos Blancos! or Welcome White People!* (Alex Torra), the apology delivered by the group Veterans Stand with Standing Rock during protests against the Dakota Access Pipeline, and Kukuli Velarde's body of work, from *We, The Colonized Ones* to *A mi vida*. This book visualizes empathy as an affective response grounded in subjectivity and kinship. Following recent work on empathy by Lanzoni, Maibom, Bloom, Hogan, and Matravers, among others, I examine in-group/out-group divisions and the establishment of identity categories through performance.

The selection of performances does not pretend to inform the history of an era. Its time period, nonetheless, is contained, or suspended from two edges, like a bridge. In 1992, the widespread celebrations of the quincentenary anniversary of the Spanish Conquest enterprise resurrected dialog and debate about the "collective memory of colonial violence in America."[5] Nao Bustamante and Kukuli Velarde were among the many artists that felt compelled to engage in this dialog. At the same time, 1992 marks the occasion when in reaction to the acquittal of three of the four policemen involved in the beating of an unarmed black man called Rodney King, Los Angeles broke out into five days of violence. This was the first case of US police brutality to be filmed and widely televised both nationally and internationally. Anthony Lewis's essay titled "Abroad at Home: A Lost Country," published in the *New York Times*, aptly presented the sense of disorientation this incident stirred.[6] In New York, in Washington Heights, the death of the Dominican Kiko García spurred similar protests in response to police brutality. *Dominicanish* (1999) by Josefina Báez includes audiovisual material about these riots happening in response to this killing. With the turn of the century and the end of the Cold War, the US fought fewer enemies beyond its borders, but according to the historian Michael Sherry, "the fewer enemies the United States found beyond its borders, the more it found within them."[7] Meanwhile, as a more "profound understanding of American cultural hybridity called for redefinitions of national identity and national origins," subjects belonging or standing at the crossroads of two kinship positions began to claim stage space in performance.[8] Josefina Báez waited no time to claim this space, and neither did Nao Bustamante.

With Obama's visit to Cuba in 2016, the Cold War era seemed ready to be melted, once again. As with the effervescence caused by the Buena Vista Social Club project, exchanges between the nations began to sprout everywhere—Cuban artists, writers, intellectuals, historians, etc., were on the agendas of all academic institutions. When Cuba–US relations warmed up, Cuban-Americans began yet again to think about the cultural hybridity of what Gustavo Pérez Firmat calls a life on the hyphen.[9] In his play *¡Bienvenidos Blancos! or Welcome White People!* Alex Torra explores the feeling of inhabiting two kinship positions and the attempts to think about how he responds to out-group and in-group relations as a gay white Cuban-American. That same year marked the deadliest mass shooting in US history targeting LGBTQ people. On June 12, 2016, a gunman opened fire in a gay nightclub in Orlando. Also in 2016, from April to December, thousands of protesters gathered at Standing Rock to support Indigenous opposition to the Dakota Access Pipeline near the Standing Rock Indian Reservation. Among them, was the organization Veterans Stand, co-founded by Michael Wood, who worked as a policeman for eleven years and became known for speaking out against police brutality.[10] The protest, and the type of response it encountered, made apparent that colonial violence was not a thing from a distant past; the conquest and its aftermath were once again, as in 1992, begging not to be celebrated. Through art and performance, Kukuli Velarde and Veterans Stand with Standing Rock stated clearly their positions about these issues.

Since 2015, but particularly in 2020, this collective memory of colonial violence in America was revisited. In response to the killing of George Floyd, the Black Lives Matter movement massively sparked numerous events and protests in the midst of a pandemic. There has been since an accompanying epidemic of hate crimes and mass-shootings. In 2019, while large caravans of asylum seekers kept arriving to the border, a gunman opened fire at an El Paso Walmart targeting Latinos "in response to the Hispanic invasion of Texas"[11] George Floyd's choking seemed to show that nothing had changed since the beating of Rodney King, but in-group and out-group relations were once again revisited as the protests that occurred all around the nation seemed to imply that White America was massively reckoning with systemic racism. Privilege and dis-privilege needed to be thought in tandem, and Alex Torra and Kukuli Velarde planned to do that.

Just around the time Kukuli's long postponed performance was about to take place, yet another mass shooting happened, in Uvalde, Texas, where nineteen children and two teachers died at Robb Elementary School. Kukuli had initially conceived her ceramic babies installation with the five thousand migrant families forcibly separated at the border from their children during the Trump administration in mind. Yet, the massacre at Robb Elementary School in Uvalde, Texas, perpetrated by a Latino man on Latinos, mostly children, affected her, Kukuli stated, because the show was dedicated to her daughter, then in elementary school.

In closing, these events, which further mobilized reflection on in-group and out-group relations and/or the place of Latinxs in the US racial American landscape, prompted Nao Bustamante, Josefina Báez, Alex Torra, Kukuli Velarde, and Veterans Stand to grapple with this array of issues, while rehearsing their performances of identity. Presenting these artistic enactments in the context of a period that goes from the 500-anniversary celebration of the Spanish conquest to the Black Lives Matter movement in the US helps to inform the historical construct of boundaries and bodies in performances of identity. Exploring performances of identity at the boundaries of two kinship positions (which vary from case to case) serves, initially, to situate the place of Latinxs in the US racial American landscape. But most importantly, it presents a corpus of performances that link "power" and "otherness" in a manner that neither celebrates the magic power of "subversion" nor eschews any attempt for more equitable models of exchange. I focus on enactments of power in performance that an "other" builds, but my emphasis is not on deconstructing the construction of ethnic bodies. My approach seeks to be more critically constructive than destructive. I engage with different aspects of empathic thought in performance, because this medium "acknowledges the present moment of exchange between embodied participants, embedded in cultural codes."[12] This work seeks to perform a specific type of scholarship in which critics belonging to underrepresented actors count not only as objects of study but also as subjects providing epistemic frameworks and theoretical concerns. For that reason, Hortense Spillers, José E. Muñoz, Ngugi wa Thiong'o, and Gloria Anzaldúa provide the four theoretical pillars upon which each chapter stands, aided by works from Lorgia García Peña, Odette Casamayor-Cisneros, Carolyn Calloway-Thomas, and Adrian Piper.

Empathy entails, as one of its main elements, a notion of the other. All the performances analyzed here postulate a relationship between the self and the other. They also pose a relational situation that either repairs, cleanses, or contests identity categorizations as points of departure to demand, puzzle, explore, or exhibit empathy. The different chapters will address these last four scenarios. Thinking of empathy *in* performance and *as* performance bridges the gap between the spatial dimension of empathy—to dwell in another's place—and its epistemic conditions of possibility. Perception can be rehearsed to regularly include other, less powerful subject positions within our personal space of concern. Through this book we will take different aspects into account; each chapter is like a new rehearsal session.

We tend to think that empathy happens "inside" of us and moves outward, toward the object that elicits it, but the object (and its inner and outer space) are read with the letters of an alphabet that is neither universal nor personal. This research brings to the fore the epistemic significance of emotions in performance and the need to visualize emotional dispositions in cultural criticism. The selected performances seek care for the hedonic state of the self or other and, in this realm, set the conditions of possibility for empathic thought. The language of enactments of power employs or implies identity categories that can enhance or inhibit fellow feelings. The epistemic power of performance, I argue, rests not on reflecting on the American experience of otherness but on moving toward understanding some aspects of this experience.[13] The act of understanding through empathic thought makes use of previous reflections to form new associations between emotions and experience. One can read all one's life about racism or bigotry, but actually going through the experience of it casts a bright light on its shadows. It is here that, following Patrick Hogan, I will distinguish between spontaneous and elaborative empathy.

Empathy as an elaborated emotion encompasses various sources of information that don't simply derive from emotional systems. Working memory produces new imaginations, reconstructs episodic memories, and activates emotional memories by integrating new, incoming information from perception and memory. These processes constitute emotional elaboration, where perception, imagination, and memories act collectively.[14] Elaborative empathy is trained through a critical take on forms of interaction.[15]

In this selection of performances interaction is a form of intervention; it happens on stage, on expectations, during rehearsals, and on the staged gaze. The power of a performance to spur empathy, rests not only in enabling openness to the experience of parallel emotions (that is, spontaneous empathy), but also in cultivating the skills to "attend, categorize, simulate, and model the other person's emotional experience."[16] Empathy is an emotion that brings together notions of interiority and exteriority in more than one realm (body, identity, form of life, history).[17] Elaborative empathy also entails an assessment of intentions and actions, which goes beyond the realm of automatic emotional responses. In the following chapters, I will explore five performances: *Indigurrito*, which took the mandate of commemorating the conquest to enact something quite different; *Dominicanish*, which defied expectations placed on Black and Latina bodies through a sustained tension between body and verbal language; *¡Bienvenidos Blancos! or Welcome White People!*, a play articulating the position of feeling both brown and white; and, finally, an apology that performs the acknowledgment of unjust oppression that Gloria Anzaldúa demanded from white gringos considered alongside Kukuli Velarde's work, which revisits Anzaldúa's interpellation through ceramic sculptures and painting.

This will allow us to begin and end with enactments of power that mirror each other and consider the differential Ngũgĩ wa Thiong'o posed between the power of performance in the arts and the performance of power.[18] Since one of the main elements of empathy is the notion of an "other," these performances are a way of accessing previous epistemic conditions about what the self that is not "other" owes to the other and, conversely, what representations subjects in the position of "other" pose as empowering. In short, what do the powerful owe to subjects outside this position of power? How is this imbalance addressed? What forms of relationship between self and other are postulated? These are all questions we will explore to address the relationship between identity, structures of knowledge, and empathy in performance.

Just as performance considered itself from its inception as breaking the fourth wall of theater, so too did empathy in its proposed shift away from sympathy: simply put, empathy entails "feeling with" as opposed to "feeling for." Empathy appeared in culture when more traditional, Victorian terms for feeling, such as sympathy or sentiment, were coming under great strain because they were seen as either claiming an unverified connection or keeping a distance from an "other." There was a desire for a new connection between minds once modern psychology began to deal with the matter of extracting evidence from other minds. This new connection sought to observe feelings in which minds think "with" each other instead of "about" each other.[19] Yet "feeling with," once in the field of neuroscience, came to demand the distinction between reverberation and recognition. The historian of emotions Ute Frevert and the social neuroscientist Tania Singer note that empathy became a fashionable research topic in the neurosciences, because, unlike the theory of mind, empathy doesn't claim "the recognition of thoughts, convictions and intentions."[20] For Frevert and Singer, "we feel empathy if 1) we find ourselves in an emotional condition, 2) this situation is isomorphic with the emotional condition of another person, 3) this condition is brought about by the emotional condition of another person, and 4) we are conscious that the other person is the trigger for 'our' condition."[21] Here it is clear that the emotional condition of an "other" affects our "selves" in a manner that elicits parallel (isomorphic) emotional responses. Emotional responses can also be complementary, as when the sense of anger in a subject generates fear or, for example, a sense of sadness brings about feelings of revenge. These are cases in which in-group/out-group relations block or mute isomorphic emotional conditions. Still, at times empathy might not be brought about fully for reasons that exceed the sort of explanation based around kinship.

Elaborative empathy is a self-conscious attempt to imagine the conditions of another person; it relies largely on concrete imagination, which is an imagining that activates perceptual regions (sensation, imagination, memory).[22] Elaborative empathy also relies on emotional memories, which often have nonrepresentational content. A highly clustered society is making it more difficult to imagine the conditions of other lives, not only because of a highly stratified way of life centered around purchasing power, but also because of a form of life that posits leadership as opposite to not-knowing, and not making mistakes. Hence, the question "What do I not know about this subject's conditions?" is actively discouraged. That is, inferential routines encourage efficiency through samples that support swift assertiveness, not the inefficient need for additional knowledge. Yet, this need is exactly the point of entry to "imagine the conditions of others." Perception is not a given—it has to be trained to come up with this inquiry when empathic inclinations are felt or demanded. The problem that the necessity of concrete imagination in empathic thought poses is that to imagine other forms of life, one has to have the experience of being in a position in which one has to function by other (unknown) rules, not precisely to experience "rules" but to weigh the dissimilar consequences of similar actions.

The capacity to infer subjective states often falls short when concrete imagination cannot be meaningfully activated. Working memory—that is, the integration of perception and memory—is guided by inferential routines. These inferential routines guide the way in which working memory identifies objects, infers causes, and constructs anticipations.[23] For example, if, when faced with the female character in "La intrusa" by J. L. Borges, our only reaction is to disdain her submissiveness, empathy is blocked because no perceptual region (sensation, memory, or imagination) about domestic violence or slavery or social oppression has been activated. Our perception is being guided by a restrictive question—roughly, "What would I do?"—instead of a broader question focused on the other: "What can this person do?" Empathy can likewise fall short when concrete imagination can be activated in only one way, independent of circumstances, for example, by holding the perception that all Mexicans are poor or that the United States is the best country in the world to live in. As we said, the way in which working memory integrates new incoming information from perception and memory is guided to a great extent by inferential routines; problematizing those inferential routines via curiosity-invoking frames will prove productive.[24]

Empathy and Teaching

What can produce the sort of epistemic curiosity in the classroom that triggers processes of elaborative empathy? Teaching opens avenues for training the imagination and fruitful debating skills, as long as it challenges inferential routines (how we explain reality and the self in it). Provisionally, one could say that this could happen if the act of teaching (a) welcomes different perspectives, (b) acknowledges and identifies a corpus of experiences and ways of life unknown to the particular audience, and (c) encourages further imagination by discouraging moral competition that accuses other perspectives of deviance without question. Unfortunately, such accusations, which often curtail empathy, are dear to a modern academic understanding of intellectual activity and "give cover to those, who, by aiming at others, can present themselves as noble and bias-free for having pointed fingers first, all of which keeps the hierarchy intact."[25] True comprehension of the other often confounds self-assertion, requiring and generating new vulnerabilities. That is why utilizing a performance as a source to explore empathic thought, one that requires imagination, care, and non-egoistic feelings, can only go as far as we ourselves are willing to go. It is a delicate balance, for although in writing, multiple points of view and lack of denunciation can be taken as comprehensive, in our teaching roles, so prone to the pressures of popularity and building definite awareness, it can come up as looking weak, confusing, lacking control, and social compromise.

A particular connection between awareness and moral superiority has obscured real efforts in understanding, in the situations in which the end game is only to avoid being labeled as ignorant, biased, racist, and so on. A society that discourages non-egoistic thought on an everyday basis does not help either. The academic paradox consists in bringing awareness to the already aware, hoping that in the midst of this, a chance encounter with the unaware occurs. Another paradox consists in equating awareness with change. Eve Sedgwick sarcastically elaborates on this point, "as though to make something visible as a problem were, if not a mere hop, skip, and jump away from getting it solved, at least self-evidently a step in that direction."[26] In the field of performance studies, Peggy Phelan fostered similar concerns, which moved her to write *Unmarked* (1993). In an interview from 2003, she echoes Sedgwick's take on the matter:

> *Unmarked* was written in the late 1980s and early 1990s. In that period in New York (and elsewhere) the Left was absolutely obsessed with identity politics and visibility politics. The idea was that if you could give the disenfranchised access to representation, these groups could secure political power. I was suspicious of this for feminist Lacanian reasons . . ., and also because I knew that this was part of what capitalism does so well—acquire new audiences! If one could increase the range of representation's demographic

addresses, capitalism could add more markets to its expanding stage. . . . I was interested in finding ways to resist the relentless acquisitive drive of capitalism.[27]

Aiming to reach the unaware might work, but we cannot ignore the fact that often we elicit an emulation of the "proper" behavior. Even appropriate phrases could be uttered without real empathic thought. I am interested in, and insist on, training the imagination for empathic thought because we need the skills to care for others. We need the training, to experience the process and the effort, even if the results do not always follow. The disposition to care for something is not automatically present; like any skill, it needs practice.

Teaching propelled my search for methods to enhance empathic thought and pushed me to unearth a set of key terms to think through the problem of empathy in performance and as performance. The classroom regularly provides performance space, or, in any case, the classroom is a performance space I can count on. For this reason, it appears at times interspersed with my analysis. Not because I claim, "these are the methods to employ," but because this is the space that generated these inquiries. The space of concern for others was regularly rehearsed and rewritten in the space of the classroom.

The role of literature in training readers to join subjectivities has been widely addressed, and we will revisit this line of research, but what remains to be thought is how the conceptual problem of other minds translates into the medium of performance. Literary works draw our attention to simulations involving systems of emotion.[28] They can give us fine-grained models of emotion, especially because emotion modeling in literature breaks free from activities that can be distracting and interactions where the ego is actively involved.[29] In performance, however, first-degree audiences are seldom left alone; instead, performance engages audiences in interaction, which strengthens the social desirability of empathy. To a great extent, "empathy self-reporting has been found to be influenced by social desirability, desire for positive evaluation, and stereotyping."[30] So, in this case, the ego, once again, is not entirely free. Sawin points to three aspects that can help theorize the nexus between self and other as it pertains to empathy and performance: "how performance constructs reciprocal positions for audience and performer, how it mobilizes desire and how it motivates investment in gendered subjective positions."[31] These three aspects relate to the epistemic power of a performance.

Audience, performer, camera, soundscape—and, in the classroom, instructor—all construct perception. Performance is an optimal medium to engage self-conscious attempts to imagine the conditions of the other person's emotional experience. Our perception deals with what the artists are doing, what the artists think/say they are doing, and what emotional conditions we imagine in this "doing." Recurring group discussions of performance geared toward expanding immediate experience can retrain inferential routines. However, this expansion of immediate experience ought to avoid taking a "conquering" approach. The result is not an incorporation of new data, with the consequent retouching of an algorithm for politically correct statements. Rather, it should be the *corporealization* of the existence of a problem not previously known.

Performance can be treated as a strategic naming of a situation. As Coco Fusco points out, performance as a discipline blurs the line between art object and body.[32] In this field, symbolic acts of difference offer a lens to view the social sphere to which this body belongs.[33] Conversely, this body allows the gaze a view of the social sphere in which otherness exists—in a discipline and in a body. On this stage of interaction, the visible aspects of the public performance bring into focus "the most acute aspects of consciousness—to perceive, to be perceived."[34] This could be called the context of otherness.

Emotions are one of the aspects that more often reveal the changing conceptions around the mind and its interiority, calling into question the apparently obvious distinction between the inner (mental) and outer (bodily) aspects of a person that informs self-understanding, and, in turn, the context of otherness.[35] We can trace the notions of interiority and exteriority, self and other, that empathy as an emotional condition carries throughout history.

The English word "empathy" first appeared in the early years of the twentieth century as a translation of the German word *Einfühlung*. *Einfühlung*, or "in-feeling," was a central concept in German aesthetics that captured the activity of transferring one's own feeling into forms and shapes of objects.[36] The term was coined by Edward Titchener (1909) as a translation of the German Einfühlung to denote an emotion that Theodore Lipps (1903) associated with understanding works of art.[37] The original concept of empathy did not incorporate the experience of the other. In the beginning there was no out-group or in-group, only the empathizer's projection. While the body has always been at the center of the discussion of emotions, in the original concept of empathy there was no "other" body and the object of our attention did not have a mind of its own. Then, once there was a subject on the other side of the relation, there was the act of understanding the other's feelings. In the end, when empathy appears in contradistinction to sympathy, the situation and the other's feelings are combined with memories of personal experience to understand not only the other's feelings but also the other's experience. If emotions pertain to an understanding of the self in the day-to-day activities of body and soul, then empathy is the specific emotion that operates to think the body and soul experience of the other. As postcolonial discourses began to progressively condemn condescending sympathetic pity, empathy as a new notion of intersubjective experience was linked to a variety of moral and epistemological ends.[38] The point was to understand experience objectively.

Measuring Empathy

Although teaching skills and processes may be more important than quantifying results, becoming familiar with current indices to measure empathy gives us a detailed view of the processes taking place in empathic thought. Maibom (2014) identifies three different routes for affective empathy: the perceptual route (witnessing), the inferential route (believing somebody is experiencing x), and the imaginative route (perspective taking).[39] The inferential route might be subdivided depending on whether the inference is based on beliefs or knowledge. Numerous studies show that feeling emotions such as disgust, fear, anger, anxiety, pleasure, embarrassment, and sadness directly (for oneself) activates brain areas that overlap with those areas that are activated when one feels the emotions for others.[40] Yet not all routes for empathy get to the same destination: empathizing with the situation (perceptual route) and empathizing in the imagination (imaginative route) have been shown to be clearly different in terms of brain activation. Maibom points out that the way in which one accesses the other's situation or emotional state is related to the type of reaction one experiences.[41]

To start with, a distinction has been made between dispositional and situational empathy. Dispositional empathy is linked to personality and character traits that are usually measured using self-report indices. Some dispositional indices measure cognitive empathy. Cognitive empathy in itself is not an emotion, but it entails skills such as "perspective taking or imaginatively engaging with others in their situation" that are also needed in affective empathy.[42] R. Hogan's Empathy Scale is one of the dispositional indices that tests cognitive empathy.[43] Brenda Bryant's index, on the other hand, tests affective empathy.[44] While the former focuses on thoughts and the latter on emotions, there are complex indices as well. Some researchers conceptualize empathy as a set of "different, but closely related emotional and cognitive capacities, and therefore construct complex indices, for example the Interpersonal Reactivity Index developed by Mark H. Davis, which measures empathy, sympathy, emotional contagion, perspective taking and fantasy."[45] This index and the Basic Empathy Scale (BES) developed by Jolliffe and Farrington measure both cognitive and affective empathy.[46] BES is not significantly influenced by social desirability, since, as the authors affirm, "a valid measure for empathy should measure a subject's empathy rather than how empathic a person wishes to be perceived."[47] In *Against Empathy*, Bloom points to the bias some tests can reinforce, from a political angle, "they measure what you think you are like, not necessarily what you are actually like. But still, they probably do capture *something* having to do with empathy, and exactly as one would predict, self-defined liberals are significantly more empathic than self-defined conservatives on both scales."[48] Most people agree that self-reports are not very reliable, but there is disagreement about whether there are better measures at hand.

Situational empathy concerns the feeling in a particular situation. Situational empathy is often evaluated in contrast to measures of situational stress to infer whether the concern is for the well-being of the other person or the self. For example, Batson's studies, employing self-reports, often use an index consisting of twenty-eight adjectives: ten characteristics of empathic concern, ten of personal distress, and eight that are neutral.[49] To supplement or substitute for these reports, researchers use physiological responses (such as skin conductivity or heart rate) and facial expressions. In the next chapter, we will see that Bustamante's "threatening interaction" tends to elicit situational stress first rather than empathetic thought. When it relates to empathic thought in response to a performance, this situational empathy can be discussed at length, although dispositional empathy would certainly make an appearance in debates about stereotypes and identity categorization.

Empathy and Power

Power shapes the experience and expression of empathy: "Those with power tend to think less of the feelings of those with less power."[50] In part, because, hierarchical structures influence how often people with power share experiences with people with no power on an egalitarian basis. Political perspectives also shape predispositions toward empathic thought and its expression. Maibom points out that conservatives might not lack empathy; rather, their empathy might be balanced, for example, with a heightened concern for moral transgressions or other issues.[51] There is a hierarchy of attention in place that plays into what constitutes moral authority and what constitutes moral transgression.

Experience became an important category of thought especially in regard to unequal relations of power. For Kenneth Clark, "empathy was not a matter of sentimentality, but a conduit to an objective understanding of the experience of those with little power."[52] The same indefatigable Kenneth Clark, together with Arthur Miller, Bayard Rustin, and Moe Foner, formed the Citizens' Inquiry on Parole and Criminal Justice that denounced and reported racism in the criminal justice system.[53] For Clark, the capacity to effect change came when people with power were able to objectively understand those with little power. That is why Clark was not interested in what he called chauvinistic empathy, a sort of empathy occurring among in-group identities.[54] Indeed, he considered it a liability. Strong in-group emotional standards might pose an obstacle to elaborative emotional responses.[55] Here, in-group empathy would react to the input of in-group demands with no elaboration or "movement"—no "dwelling into another's place."[56] Another reactive form of empathy would be what Clark denominated sentimental lies, "the tendency of whites to attribute virtue to the oppressed."[57] This does not help either, for while they might wish for the hedonic well-being of the other, they demand no understanding.

Examining contemporary discourses on ethnicity, Hortense Spillers delves further into the shortcomings of spontaneous emotional reactions when she proclaims, "under the hegemony of ethnicity the human body becomes a defenseless target for rape or veneration."[58] Soullessness, soul-body detachments and automatic virtue, despite their opposing valences, belong to the same language. The human body devoid of a soul, and therefore of the possibility of virtue, or the human body detached from a soul, which circumscribed the space of concern for others, to their "souls" but not their bodies, is a schema rehearsed in religious practices at the service of America's conquest. Denying a mind that goes beyond instinct, on the other hand, denies autonomy—virtue is then a given, not a choice. A more developed emotional condition could be what Kenneth Clark denominated "empathic reason," an emotional condition "entwining feeling and intelligence for political reform."[59] This combination of intelligence and feeling bears a close resemblance to Patrick Hogan's notion of elaborative empathy.

In regard to enactments of power, our main preoccupation is not quantifying empathic thought but unearthing key concerns around power in Latinx America from within the field of performance and identity that can translate into everyday empathic behavior. These cultural encounters could show "in what contexts empathic knowledge becomes important in the flow of human life."[60] In performance, unlike in fictional literature, the actor/author is both fictional and nonfictional. While mirror neurons might not be fired in an imaginary route to empathy, a face-to-face encounter with the performer provides just as much face-to-face encounter as in a nonfictional type of encounter. That is, the act of envisioning the auditory, visual, and bodily experiences of the character is aided by the fact that the performance provides a visual, auditory, and bodily subject/object of attention onstage—the point of view of the author/actor in these performances is close to explicit.

Structure of This Book

Each chapter in this book traces different aspects of rehearsing elaborative empathy skills by analyzing the novel interactions created through performance. I am grateful for the extensive time that Nao Bustamante, Josefina Báez, Alex Torra, Jenna Horton, Benjamin Camp, Jorge Caballero, Kukuli Velarde, and Levi Rickert generously shared with me, and I've integrated materials from my interviews with them throughout the book.

The first chapter is a study of *Indigurrito* by Nao Bustamante. By analyzing the "ritual purification" presented on stage, it shows how identity categories influence different, and at times contradictory, readings of enactments of power in ways that enhance or obstruct an empathic response. The methodological lens for this chapter borrows from Hortense Spillers's notion of "flesh" to analyze how interaction is staged and the role assigned to the Latina body. "Flesh" is a concept developed by Spillers to denote a zero degree of social conceptualization: "the concentration of 'ethnicity' that contemporary critical discourses neither acknowledge nor discourse away."[61] The study is also informed by the tenets of a theory in the flesh, as understood by Cherríe Moraga. For Moraga, a theory in the flesh entailed naming her collective history and refusing an easy explanation of the struggles. For her, entering the lives of others required acknowledging the physical realities of a lived experience, attending to those voices that bridge the lived contradictions of their bodily experiences: "This is how our theory develops," by telling "our own stories in our own words."[62] I believe these two takes on flesh resonate with each other when it comes to a performance commemorating the five hundredth anniversary of the conquest of America. After analyzing the perspectives of different kinds of subject positions both by the author/actor and by the audience/participants, I consider the possibility of elaborative empathy. One of its elements, identity categorization, influences not only openness to parallel emotions but also skills at understanding other people's emotional experiences.[63]

The second chapter offers an analysis of *Dominicanish* by Josefina Báez. Unlike Bustamante, Báez neither explains nor resolves the tension between self and other. The piece explores emotional memories by playing with different forms of tension between body language and verbal language. As an Afro-Latina, Báez defies the status quo while at the same time performing a gentle type of dis-identification. This chapter introduces this term, as understood by both Michel Pêcheux and José Esteban Muñoz, and it will be further explored in the third chapter. The theoretical analysis of *Dominicanish* puts Báez's artistic choices in conversation with Odette Casamayor-Cisneros's notion of occurrence, Patricia Hill Collins's concept of standpoints, and Adrian Piper's reflections on "art as catalysis," in which the critic elaborates on the impact of the artist using the plastic possibilities of her own body.

The final two chapters study enactments of power and the problem of other minds in contexts of intercultural understanding (Calloway-Thomas).[64] The third chapter focuses on the theater play *¡Bienvenidos Blancos! or Welcome White People!* to examine how feelings entail subject positions, paying specific attention to the "commons of the brown" that José Esteban Muñoz posed in contraposition to white affect, where the "commons" refers to a theoretical and practical attempt to think spaces of interaction outside the privatization of social life and global capitalism, and "brown," refers to the negative space of whiteness. The play explores emotional experiences attached to Cubanness and exile, which are often loaded with additional layers of conflictive memories. Through the four parts of the play, actors, crafting the piece collectively, diagram subject positions of their own. The play allows the director to disidentify with past prejudices and collaborate with subjects raised under dissimilar ideological positions.

The final chapter takes up enactments of disempowerment. I analyze the apology delivered by Veterans Stand with Standing Rock at protests against the Dakota Access Pipeline— which put people with a military background on both sides of the protest— setting it in conversation with the notion of anticolonial entropy through the study of Kukuli Velarde's work. I also consider the violence accompanying contact zones by focusing on psychic borderlands, which make visible the emotional labor that occurs during the apology act. Playing with the figure of the loop, this chapter analyzes an apology in which a white man kneels in a sort of ritual purification, much like that in *Indigurrito*, but this time not posed as performance art. The loop also serves a theoretical purpose, given that I revisit Anzaldúa's interpellation of the white man and her demand that acts of physical and psychological violence be acknowledged.[65] Kukuli Velarde's *Daddy Likee?*, a painting acquired by the Pennsylvania Academy of Fine Arts in 2019, actively interpellates the viewer, acknowledging different types of psychological violence she encountered. The opening of Velarde's first solo painting show in 2018, where *Daddy Likee?* took center stage, included a performance employing some of her ceramic sculptures. She was in the process of creating those for another future installation and performance, which took place in 2022. In both events, she combined a rich heritage of pre-Columbian cultures with current issues. Velarde's attention to her pre-Columbian cultural heritage aims to disempower the hegemony of Western aesthetics and ways of seeing. Here, the relationship of the body to a body of knowledge reemerges.

The resulting integrated framework seeks to highlight some crucial processes that structure understanding of other people's experience, perhaps, to demand more of these rehearsals, that envision other forms of feeling. In a very definitive sense, the analysis that here unfolds is my own performance. The readers might engage with what they judge fruitful and/or stimulating, while thinking their own personal points of departure to demand, puzzle, explore, or exhibit empathy.

1

Empathy and Flesh in Performance

I PRESENT HERE a study of the performance *Indigurrito* by Nao Bustamante to show how perceived identity categories and perceived intentions influence different, at times contradictory, readings of enactments of power that could enhance or obstruct an empathic response. Empathy is here a tool, a technique, a practice, and an aspiration.[1] As Lanzoni suggests, empathy points toward a comprehensive grasp of somebody's experience—that is, the ability to engage with a variety of feelings and inhabit, sometimes even bodily, the other's perspective.[2] This carries a spatial dimension— the ability to dwell in another's place and to see from this vantage point, which, however, can vary according to the medium.[3] Rivera, in a 2014 presentation at a Platform summit, spoke about movie heroes who are celebrated for breaking boundaries and the law to get to a better place, while immigrants are deemed "illegal aliens" and demonized: "It soon became clear to me that what is celebrated in science fiction is criminalized in reality."[4] As Hortense Spillers points out, "This economy of narrative means dwarfs the background and its particularities, as the 'hero' is dramatically foregrounded at all costs."[5] This economy of narrative means signals toward two facts: enactments of power are conceived differently according to subject position, and imaginaries are liberated differently depending on their relative distance from actions and participatory behavior. Thinking of empathy in performance and as performance bridges the gap between the spatial dimension—to dwell in another's place—and its epistemic conditions of possibility.

Hortense Spillers's notions of flesh and kinship provide a framework for analyzing the "stage of interaction" between bodies and the Latinx body. Before a subject position that is a site of prescribed degradation (a captive body), Spillers claims, there is flesh, the zero degree of social conceptualization, a liberated subject position still conceptualized and concealed by discourse and iconography.[6] Skin pigmentation determined the measure of humanity bestowed upon bodies. In this common historical ground, flesh points to a particular mechanism of cultural unmaking and an ongoing objectification within the new world.[7] Isabel Wilkerson describes this cultural unmaking, "Each Immigrant arriving to this new world had to figure out how and where to position themselves in the hierarchy of their adopted new land. Oppressed people from around the world . . . shed their old selves, and often their own names to gain admittance to the powerful dominant majority."[8] This, Spillers calls an "American grammar." In the sociopolitical order of the New World, "the body becomes a territory of cultural and political maneuver."[9]

For Moraga, "a theory in the flesh means one where the physical realities of our lives—our skin color, the land or concrete we grew up on, our sexual longings—all fuse to create a politic born out of necessity."[10] "Necessity" here refers to a situation in which there is a need to "bridge the contradictions in our experience."[11] It is also understood that theory, not in the flesh, does not account for the day to day of othered bodies in America. The question arising from these considerations is where we locate the idea of "the flesh." What is "flesh" in our culture?

There is a national hierarchy of bodies that renders the Latino an extra-national body yet at the same time "gives it a central role while negotiat[ing] the possibilities for national belonging during pivotal crisis moments in American cultural history."[12] The Latina body traces in parallel the social construct of that which is designated as "feminine" and the position of Latinos in a national hierarchy of bodies. As a "flesh-and-blood entity" (Spillers) the Latinx body lends itself to historical enactments that negotiate systems of devaluation that render them outside the national; at the same time these bodies are part of a landscape where exploring the exterior of American morals is possible. These ethnically marked bodies are given access to America's melting pot so long as they reenact difference in the flesh; the concentration of ethnicity serves here, as Spillers notes, to mute America's involvement in the narratives of the Caliban (imperialism and slave trade), underscoring liberty instead.[13] This stage of interaction can provide a starting place to think through how Bustamante's body becomes a territory of cultural and political maneuver.

Bustamante's long trajectory encompasses performance art, video installation, visual art, filmmaking, and writing. The tricks for using her body that McGarry (2009) once mentioned[14] include duct-taping legs to elevate her bottom, using ladders to achieve different angles of view, and exploring the grotesque and the heterotopic. "Heterotopies" were a notion elaborated by Foucault around 1967 to describe real spaces that create virtual ones, spaces that have more layers of meaning and contribute to creating another location for the self.[15] Overall, Bustamante's works deal with different heterotopic environments; the dysphoric and ludic are often present in tandem. Apart from *Indigurrito*, two other performances deal with American affairs. One of them is *America the Beautiful*, in which the artist, naked, performs a satire of Marilyn Monroe's type of sexiness, and this act of ridicule sparks the audience's laughter. The other, *Sans Gravity*, is one of her most political and refers to waterboarding. In it, Nao dips her head into a bag full of water that is later tied to her neck, holding her breath until she can no longer breathe. She did this one in Sweden in 1998 and at Tisch NYU in 2003, where it was adapted to add numerous bags to surround her body in a sort of Michelin-tire-man body shape. It did somehow in this way lose gravitas, because focusing only on the head clearly related to a form of torture carried out by US forces: waterboarding. *Indigurrito* is one of the few performances in which audience

participation was needed for the performance to happen. Moreover, this interaction happened on stage and posed an enactment
of power presented as a ritual of purification. Of all Bustamante's
performances dealing with political affairs in the Americas, this
one combines the deliberate use of the body as artistic tool and an
enactment of power as political commentary.

Indigurrito was performed in May 1992 at San Francisco's Theater Artaud, a performance lab run by a friend of Bustamante, who
lived ten blocks away from the theater at the time.[16] The event's official blurb, archived at the Hemispheric Institute of Performance,
presents it as follows:

> *Indigurrito* is Nao Bustamante's contribution to the many perfor-
> mances that commemorated the 500 anniversary of the conquest
> of America. The title mixes the term "indigenous" with "burrito,"
> the name of the famous Mexican wrap. In the performance, Busta-
> mante challenged the white men in the audience to go onstage to
> express their apologies for the years of oppression of indigenous
> peoples by eating a piece of a burrito that Bustamante had strapped
> on to her hips. With humor and sarcasm, Bustamante addressed
> the issues that the 500-year commemoration brought to collective
> attention. Her piece also denounces how art institutions forced
> artists to pay tribute to the date if they wanted to get funding.[17]

The fact that the burrito is not originally Mexican food but an American invention that was very popular in San Francisco adds still
another layer of sarcasm to the representation of the "indigenous."
As noted, *Indigurrito* is a response to the guidelines for the commemoration of the conquest of America, which Bustamante states
required her to "complete a performance based on five hundred
years of repression in order to get funded." She interprets the brief,
placing a burrito between her legs and inviting white men to "take
the burden of five hundred years of guilt." As one by one they take a
bite of burrito, they say their name and why they are there. Some are
there to humor the performer and help the performance happen;
others are there for the "burrito," interested in the proposed "ritual

of purification." The burden acts as an ambiguous penance, which plays on the burden of delight as well, but does not really move the Latina woman out of the light of sexualized object of desire. The performance breaks with the duality of the sacred and the sexual fundamental to Western guilt, but the description of the motives of the staged act do not debunk the fact that the Latina woman is once again the hypersexualized flesh upon which the white body explores a place of disinhibition as a heterotopia where Western mores don't apply. And yet, San Francisco was then a place where the queer community dealt with Western mores differently.

In *On Making Sense*, Ernesto Javier Martínez shows that "Queer Latina/o writers and theorists in the 1980 and 1990s found themselves in contexts (often violent) where the logic of 'migration-as-emancipation' came into crisis but still had purchase for them as queer racialized subjects, not as an idealized route toward 'freedom,' but as a counterhegemonic acknowledgment that they were negotiating new subjectivities and knowledge through the very act of surviving collectivities through movement."[18] This spatial dimension, in conjunction with identity categories, creates in-group and out-group relations, the self and the other. It is here that the inner and outer space of the soul that Scheer traces in "Topographies of Emotion" translates into the inner and outer space of in-group/out-group experiences. Scheer discusses introverted devotional practices that explored, mapped, and named the inner spaces of the soul. Enactments of power that request or elicit empathy do the same in terms of the outer space of the self. Empathy is an emotion that brings together notions of interiority and exteriority, as do many other emotions, but it does so within the space of concern for others. The location of the "other" within our space of concern, like boundaries, has fluid interiorities and exteriorities that, as Febvre noted, are historical, not natural.[19] The ritual of purification that *Indigurrito* reenacts reveals different emotional boundaries in the space of concern for others.

Indigurrito begins when Bustamante enters the stage dressed in very little and holding a small rectangular tray, which she puts down on the floor, giving a sort of cameo of her buttocks, saying,

FIGURE 1.1 Scene from *Indigurrito* by Nao Bustamante, producer, creator. Audience participants who reported to the stage waiting for the invitation to take the burden of the last five hundred years of guilt. May 1992 at the Theatre Artaud, San Francisco, California.

"That might have been the highlight of the next ten minutes." Then she proceeds to introduce the "origins" of the piece: "I was told this year that any artist of color must complete a performance based on five hundred years of repression in order to get funded, so this is my version." What follows is the presentation of the burrito—we learn that is what is on the tray—as "the representation of the modern indigenous people," in Nao's words. Heavy breathing prepares her and the audience to receive the participatory activity, *the invitation*, which gives form to the performance. She notes that she would like to think of her performance not as audience participation so much as audience salvation. The invitation, "I'd like to ask any white man who would like to take the burden of the last five hundred years of guilt to report to the stage now," is progressively rephrased to finally gather the support of enough participants. Beforehand, Bustamante had asked two of her friends (the fifth and seventh participants, a dancer and an illustrator) to come up in case nobody did; she did not know the rest of the participants.[20]

Before installing the burrito in the harness between her legs, she serves the seven participants an appetizer. While everybody claps and laughs, she finishes putting on the burrito and then hushes them, saying, "I only have ten minutes." The ambience is collegial, and she treats them like a group of unruly kids who might be her friends. The people on stage are then asked to kneel to prepare themselves for the cleansing that "you are about to receive." She notes, "Nothing makes me happier than people kneeling to bite a burrito," and then says, "Anyone who is offended by this, I really encourage you to just leave your body." She invites each participant to say their name, any name they want, and make a statement before absolving themselves, adding, "I just want to encourage you to feel the healing rush that is going to surge through your body as you take the guilt for all those people that were too much of a coward to come up onstage, 'cause everybody will be channeling all their shit right into your body. You know that, right?" The audience is instructed to say "a man" as each man's teeth bite into the burrito. "A man; not amen, but a man." What follows could be taken as the play within the play:

FIRST MAN:

__My name is Marty. There are few things that can give me more pleasure than biting into your burrito.

__A man

SECOND MAN:

__I am Justin. I am male, I am white, I am sorry.

__A man

THIRD MAN:

__I am Paul, Saint Paul, and I do this for all.

__A man

FOURTH MAN:

__I am . . . Olive . . . Philips. Thank you from all of my people; we need this so much.

__ A man.

FIFTH MAN:

__ I am Allen. I just want to say I am sorry too.

__A man

SIXTH MAN:

__ My name is Patrick. For all the Catholics in the audience, this should be your [first] confession.

__ A man

SEVENTH PERSON:

__ I am a girl, I am Hispanic, and I am prepared. [She tries to put a condom on the by-now-disintegrating burrito.]

__ A woman

And with that, the piece is finished. Nao thanks everyone for taking the brunt of the guilt and for supporting theater.

The idea for the performance and how it came about speaks of a particular community and era:

The city was launching different kinds of cultural programs about this issue, and so it was a response to that, but also just, you know, silliness. Like I had a friend who ran a performance lab. He was a poet, he invited me, and I said, I come and I wear my strap-on burrito, and we just laughed 'cause you know, burritos were so iconic in San Francisco as a food object, and then I worked at this women and sex toys store called Good Vibrations.[21] So, there was this kind of mashup in my mind of these things. And then we laughed so much about this that then I said, "We should do this somehow for a performance." Much of my work happens with a kind of image that pops up into my head. That is kind of how it came about, and then the audience was very dynamic and excited, and there were probably a lot of artists in the audience. It was kind of a hometown audience. It was this yearly show that they did.[22]

Following a 2002 interview where Bustamante stated she wanted to poke fun at "la raza," "hardcore feminist theory," and "ritual performance art," Leticia Alvarado considers that Bustamante developed "this sentiment into the performance *Indigurrito*."[23] There is no doubt Bustamante still "recognized that she had been invited to perform her minoritized identity," but during my 2019 interview she chose to highlight other aspects of what mobilized her and other "sentiments."[24] According to José Esteban Muñoz, "Bustamante's body illuminates a particular predicament around agency within the social: a feeling queer, a feeling brown, that is both about belonging and the failure to belong."[25] For Alvarado many Bustamante's performances provide a reflection on minority inclusion; I would like to supplement this reading with one that envisions a performance of belonging, but at the same time asks: which minority's inclusion?[26]

Indigurrito illustrates how the perception of different political bodies features considerations about identity that are deemed as near or distant to a space of concern for others that is recognized or valued. Spillers has pointed out that feelings of kinship describe in-depth relationships that, although they look natural, are cultivated under actual material conditions.[27] For Spillers, the "metaphysics of the social and political body" are not about one element, feature, or identity, but about settling for an arbitrary parameter to determine "near" and "far," "inner" and "outer," "licit" and "illicit."[28] The context of emotions has a liminal space that belongs to perception. "Flesh," a concept developed by Spillers to denote the zero degree of social conceptualization, informs the blind spots of context, so to speak, the standard behaviors one does not question.[29] For Spillers, representations point to actions on the stage of life, and this work echoes her theoretical gesture. There is "a specific type of sociability" that Avery Gordon asserts, "draws us affectively into the structure of feeling of a reality we come to experience not as cold knowledge but as transformative recognition."[30] A question to ask would be: What types of transformations can we recognize? Can those be sought after?

As Bustamante's career progressed, she began to direct video performances, and used nudity less often as an expressive tool, yet she still highly praises it as an artistic choice:

> Because my body doesn't fit into the realm of what would be a contemporary fit body, I think it must have the reaction on people, where they must say, "Wow, she is so brave." They immediately

then have to question their own judgment, that is: what is so brave about me showing my body? It functions on a lot of different levels when you show your body to people. . . . Everybody's own bodies are kind of all we have beyond our own minds and how we can think *outside* of our own bodies. I feel brave. I am not sure if I feel empowered, but I do feel *brave and I do feel the power of it.* I feel like the space of my body takes up not just around my skin but in the type of psyche of others.[31]

Here the space of the body goes beyond "skin," just as flesh always does, "in the psyche of others." The relation Bustamante establishes between the body and the possibility of thinking "outside our own bodies" is telling; it feels like the idea of thinking outside the box. Yet, when in the performance she urges "those who feel offended just leave your body" the proposed reaction, "just leave your body" could also speak of trauma or gender dysphoria. Stephanie Burt in a recent book review quotes from the novel *Nevada*, "The moment her pants come off, she stops being in her body," and adds, "That is how sex feels when you don't think your body is yours."[32]

By analyzing the perspectives of the author/actor and the audience/participants, I consider the possibility of elaborative empathy—the voluntary attempt to imagine "the other person's emotional experience."[33] Here I focus on one element of elaborative empathy, identity categorization. In the case of *Indigurrito*, this aspect influences openness to parallel emotions and is tied to skills in understanding another person's emotional experience. This means that faced with subjects who hold more than one identity, identity categorization might perceive or privilege one more than another, affecting what we can imagine and what we can understand. The array of reactions to *Indigurrito* will make concrete this rather abstract idea.

Since the performance presents itself as an enactment of power, we ought to consider the reading of power in relation to empathy and the multiple subject locations in the performance: those of the author, the participant actors, and the viewers. Having access to the author's perspective allows us to contrast the intentions that we attribute to the author through our empathic response to the intentions actually expressed by the author. In other words, it permits us to contrast the assumed logic with the expressed logic. The inclusion of the artist's voice is crucial to learn what is empowering for her. This last step is necessary to move from empathizing abstractly with an identity category to relating to a unique real person in that identity category. Problem solving, imagining consequences, and leaving space to hear that "this does not represent me" or "this is not empowering to me" statements permit a more nuanced grasp of what is at stake in enactments of power as they relate to empathy. Eliciting empathy is always a desired outcome, but nurturing elaborative empathy depends greatly on the act of facilitating it by training the necessary cognitive and socio-psychological skills. In *Indigurrito*, Bustamante is both author and actor, so one can reconstruct the performance to study it as a happening (an event score) and as an action. With the inclusion of a second-degree audience— the students and artists who later watch the filmed performance— one can pivot a further step back and rethink the event as text to see how language works, what can be said with it and what cannot.

For Nao, this work is basically about two things: power differentials and mechanisms for moving beyond those power differentials.[34] Bustamante's upbringing, according to her, established a special relationship with punishment that affects how she deals with power differentials: "This idea that you are being punished so that you can relieve yourself is very Catholic . . . the idea of guilt: punish yourself and then you feel better. Guilt is part of a mechanism shaping empowerment here. I grew up with that kind of idea, and I did punish myself a lot. As a child, for my thoughts, or something, people would punish me, yet I would punish myself even more than they had punished me. It is like a way of manipulating people."[35] In this performance that could be deemed a spectacle of punishment as simulacrum, guilt is mentioned, but shame is challenged.

In *Indigurrito* Nao Bustamante chooses iconoclasm as a source of empowerment. Religion is a paradigmatic example of something that can empower and oppress different communities. The emotional memories activated by some individuals might encompass boredom, repression, self-doubt, harassment, a sense of community, a sense of alienation, self-affirmation, emotional abuse, solidarity, and more. The condition one thinks the individual is in will be affected by these unconscious inferences, as well as by inferential routines in the description and explanation of emotional experiences and development—in short, what we are predisposed to perceive and how we do explain perceptions. The social consideration of sexuality might encounter divergent responses as well. For certain communities, it might be liberatory to refrain from an overt expression of sexual desire and behavior. For others, it might be just the opposite: their expression would be a way of breaking taboos. What counts as "overt expression" also differs. What in one culture is an outrageous declaration might just be business as usual in another. Our capacity to infer subjective states will be highly informed by these epistemic habits of meaning.

The integration of perception and memory can work in very different ways; for example, in the case of *Indigurrito*, one may identify a white man as the main object of attention, or may identify the performer as the main object of attention. Yet, the anticipations constructed around actions and speech vary not only according to the prioritized object of attention and emotional concern, but also by the object of attention the performance constructs, since our response is being observed by peers around us (outer space) and is being informed by social norms of proper thought (inner space).

Flesh and Enactments of Power

For Ngũgĩ wa Thiong'o, the performance space is always a site of physical, social, and psychic forces in society.[36] The magic and power of performance comes from the fact that the entire space becomes a magnetic field of tensions and conflicts. The space is eventually transformed into a sphere of power revolving around its own axis like a planet in outer space. But, the magic is not suspended in total isolation. There are other centers and fields of human action.[37] Ngũgĩ places his analysis within the reality of National Kenyan

Theatre thirteen years after Kenya's formal independence in 1976, and on an occasion in which Kenya was going to host a UNESCO general conference.[38] In "Enactments of Power: The Politics of Performance Space," Ngũgĩ wa Thiong'o proposes to look at the performance space of the artist. Ngũgĩ contraposes the performance space of the artist with the state's own areas of performance. Enactments of power emerge from a rivalry between the state and the artist. Since the domain of culture has always embodied the desirable and the undesirable in the realm of values, expressed through performance, state and artist compete in articulating the prevailing laws, moral and formal, and in determining the manner and circumstances of their delivery.[39] Censorship is an obvious way in which the state seeks to deter certain manners of delivery, but funding is just another way of determining it. Bustamante plays with the tensions involved in enactments of power, but inside a different set of forces. The ways and means of negotiating borders and center was becoming, in 1992, a new area of studies in the liberal arts curriculum, one that professor Valerie Smith called "doing otherness."[40]

Taking Spillers's notion of flesh, I want to look at the performance space of the artist's flesh. That borrows from Ngũgĩ's notion of performance space as a site of physical, social, and psychic forces in society, but narrows down the space to the artist's flesh. There is a petition for representations of difference that is all too familiar to enactments of power performed by "others" in America, but we need to observe *the* perceived empowerments and *the* particular lack(s) of power that are performed and represented. In "Who Cuts the Border? Some Readings on America," Spillers examines otherness as represented by the figure of Caliban in English literature. She delineates an "other America" in response to José Martí's "Our America" and discusses the "contradictions of proximity" and "overdetermined representability."[41] For Spillers, "Colonial North America muted its involvements in the narratives of Caliban . . . by the fateful creation of 'minority' communities in the US, but it is the ascribed task of such minorities to keep the story of difference under wraps through the enactment and reenactment of difference in the flesh."[42] This petition for representation of difference *in the flesh* marks the flesh's entrance into the space of performance. Spillers clarifies the problematic nature of the liberated subject position, or flesh, that she opposes to the captive body. Going back to *Indigurrito*, we can observe that while the "modern indigenous people(s)" presented as "the burrito" are there to feed and give pleasure, the performer's task is to authorize a ritual of purification that cleanses "guilt." For Bustamante, guilt has a sort of buffering *dispositif* tucked inside—a very convoluted but at the same time a logical one that inspires a sarcastic approach to power:[43]

> The idea, you know, eye for an eye, tooth for a tooth, comes into play. So, can I wipe away five hundred years of oppression through this action? And, then as a way of sort of sweetening the idea, can I wipe away your guilt? From the oppressor . . . and would that free me? You know, would you take your foot out of my neck if you don't feel guilty anymore?
>
> *So if white people stop being guilty they can stop being as oppressive. . .*
>
> Yeah, because then they can start thinking about it . . . it is sort of like your foot is on my neck and you are going . . . "Am I still oppressing you? My foot is oppressing you . . . is it possible that I am an oppressor? But it is not me, that is not who I am.[44]

In the present, inequalities and injustices are "tucked" inside icons and traditions. When empowerment adopts iconoclasm, it is often read as an attack on traditions and peace, not on injustice. Although our analysis of *Indigurrito* could consider the US state in 1992, when the performance is used in the classroom it responds to more immediate performances of power in the university, such as funding, cultural programs, mission statements, and clients, boards of trustees, and so forth, as well as all the other events happening at the time that relate to repression and demands for social justice. Enactments of power are, therefore, defined as the struggle between the power of performance in the arts and the performance of power by the state, just as in Ngũgĩ's analysis, but the scale varies. The performance of power in the theater or in the university might follow a different "funding" state of affairs, such as that Bustamante denounces, or a "public image" state of affairs, as exercised by university branding in the US. These considerations bring us close to the representability analyzed by Spillers inside the liberated subject positions posed by flesh. Bustamante uses her body as a tool to elicit responses with a clear idea of what empowerment means for her:

> A lot of times in my work, I have done this thing: I like to make people feel sorry that they laughed about something. The audience member is intricately implicated in the work or the idea or concept by virtue of participating while laughing, and then they might feel bad about themselves or question themselves why they are actually laughing. And that is a different kind of initiation. So the work is very active in that way. . . . It asks a lot, obviously, from performance, and yet I do feel there is a way in which it holds, or can hold, some kind of power, the power to express deeper psychological structures, which can freak people out, through laughter, through conversation, and so I do feel like art is, can be quiet powerful. I hold all of these things in my mind at once: I think art is kind of a scam, doesn't make any sense, is truly useless, but I don't want to live in a world that is about utility, I don't want to live in a world that is about usefulness.[45]

It could be that subjects project their inner lives onto the notion of power itself, and later this notion is reprojected, or reenacted. This "empathic reenactment," to use Greg Currie's language, as it pertains to enactments of power, might require this secondary imagining of the characters' situation in order to "extend our emotional lives into the world."[46] The tricky part about empathizing with power is that its pleasurable nature, much like beauty, might deter thoughts about its conditions of possibility and why and when empathic behavior is important. This might also affect the identification of and reflections on its significance and effectiveness, as the spectator position is ethically predisposed to take pleasure in poetic justice—the underdog getting ahead and succeeding. All this is to say that while enactments of power are proper targets for empathy, they are also targets for the pleasure of empathizing with power, so much so that one could easily project power into a situation that is, in reality, not empowering. Yet, as we noted before, for Bustamante this could be empowering: "I found that in my work, it is very powerful to make the body vulnerable. Because there is something about nakedness or vulnerability that . . . it is also about shamelessness. There is so much shame about the body, particularly about the Latina body."[47]

The problem of the experience of beauty is helpful for thinking about the problem of the experience of power. Matravers reports, following Kant, that when one says a rose is beautiful, one is in reality saying that its sight gives "me" pleasure, but were one to say the rose is beautiful *for me*, aesthetic taste would be undermined in a manner that goes contrary to the purpose of declaring "beauty."[48] The "for me" translates aesthetics into something else, less universal, clinging less to common sense. Were we to say that the performance is "powerful" or the message is powerful, adding "for me" may give the projection that goes from the mind to the object in aesthetic empathy a change of direction. Adding that this sight of power gives "me" pleasure might complicate perception even further. Empathy switches gears in contexts of power. The object/subject projects its power. Matravers rightly identifies the difference between projecting "into" and projecting "on to."[49] Projecting "on to" assumes no "identification of our self with the object."[50] LaCapra in *Understanding Others: Peoples, Animals, Pasts* highlights a similar distinction and its consequences; "incorporative or projective identification undermines understanding others by assimilating them to the self"; for him this projective identification is not empathy, which requires emotional rapport but also a certain distance and respect for the other as other.[51] He believes that empathy may be necessary but never enough for informed understanding or for viable social and political action.[52] This deterministic relation between empathy and social/political action is one of the premises that very few enactments of power in performance would be willing to let go, for it undermines the power of performance. Bluntly stated, we want to feel good and we want to be on the right side of the ethical equation; that affects expression and perception, which in turn affects how we elaborate empathy. This "beautiful for me" sounds undermining just as this "power for me" does, but in the putative exercise of empathy we want to promote, it sounds like the right approach. While empowerment exceeds and complicates "taste," it orients actions and value judgments within the social dimension of an aesthetic act.

Spillers's notion of flesh is a way of talking about the body and its liberated subject positions marked by the hegemony of ethnicity. Spillers posits flesh in opposition to bodies that are captive, but also in contrast to the idea of the natural structures of social and political bodies. Before dark flesh is considered by society as "less" than white flesh, they are both only "flesh." But "before" implies here a temporality that is tricky. Flesh, here, is the surface of a liberated position whose feelings of kinship seem natural, while in fact they are determined by arbitrary notions of "near" and "far," "inner" and "outer," "licit" and "illicit."[53]

This position, as is evident by now, is not entirely free of iconological demands and discourses that imprint upon the body features that determine what starts to count—both in terms of "self" and "other" and "in-group" and "out-group" relations that pertain to empathy, power, and identity. On the other hand, in the politics of space at stake in the performance of queer identities, "identities are not arbitrary social constructs; they obey a 'spatialization of knowledge' that, although 'harnessed' by the politics of space," allows mobilization of identificatory desires and power enactments to move.[54]

Often, identitarian needs establish the perception of a relation between two unequal identities. Elaborative empathy attempts to think about othered and less powerful identities in terms of their needs, not our own. Part of what sparked Nao Bustamante's defiant, creative move was her interest in skewing this construction of identity around the legacy of the Hispanic conquest that was directed by many "funding for the arts" grants in 1992. Whether celebrating or condemning it, funding sources intended to make this the foundational event of Hispanic, Latinx, and Chicano identities.

Bustamante, as a queer Latinx artist, understood that many different binaries could be thought at once, and power operates differently in each one: "Even then we were in that kind of intersectional space of being queer, Latina, and . . . you know, working class, and an artist, which was kind of its own identity at the time."[55]

In sum, the enactment of power I have examined must be understood as part of a subgroup, retrospectively arranged to unearth key concerns from within the wider field of performance of identity. Enactments of power vary, but primarily evoke the following:

(a) a performance of identity at the intersection of power
(b) the employment of categories of self and other that "reconfigure notions of intersubjective experience"[56]
(c) the demand for reparative action
(d) an outright denial of identity expectations and demands

Stage of Interaction

The most acute aspects of consciousness, as Spillers notes, demand the self to perceive itself while perceiving the other perceiving it.[57] The stage of interaction in *Indigurrito* sets a "paradigm for understanding the social dimension of the aesthetic act," which explains the motive, intention, and dynamic of the performance.[58] By doing this, it assigns different avenues for "white bodies" to "take the brunt of guilt."[59] The empathic subject brings about the subject outside "the self." Bustamante explains that in her daily life she likes thought, but she wants to experience feeling as well: "I have a strong belief in emotional intelligence. This kind of power that has been at times been associated with feminine power, or female energy, I think they are on the rise now, as men co-opt them into their life, or have strong experiences, or experience meaning from them."[60]

Empathy, like the "feminine" and like performance as textual production, continually evades our efforts to catch its epistemic conditions of possibility. As Rita Felski noted long ago, the key is to focus on repeated experiences rather than definitions.[61] Feminine and "othered" subjectivities often experience the sensation of being looked at, but *Indigurrito* crafts an interaction that instead *others* white men via the simulacrum of a ritual. On this account, it echoes Ann Sprinkle's performance, *Post Porn Modernism* (1989) and its flip on perspectivalism. In *Post Porn Modernism*, Sprinkle had a speculum inserted in which spectators could look at her cervix. Meanwhile, Sprinkle looked at them. As Schneider notes, "she was seeing the viewer seeing her vulva"; "distance is remarked by a gaze emanating from *within* the scopic field, not penetrating into it from without."[62] While Bustamante does not "rely on the view of the blind spot" as Schneider believes Sprinkle does, she offers a phallic strap on to devour in exchange for a flip of gazes and view heights. The perspectivalism to flip here is not the one of the woman as landscape in Duchamp's *Etant donnés*, but the moral planes established by the *dispositif* of the interrogation that penetrated America christened as confession.

In the ritual of confession that the performance echoes, the kneeling body is keenly aware of this reflection. This "othering" is halfway between the interpellation and the turn-around—what Butler (1995) calls "second timing"—between being called by an authority and responding to the call. The seven participants put themselves in a position of being looked at. The interaction does not *other* men because of this call; rather, the experience opens the possibilities of *othering* that nonetheless can be normalized if the artist were objectified. Peggy Phelan considers that moments like these reflect the potential of mutual transformation characteristic of live performance, "this potential, this seductive promise of possibility of mutual transformation is extraordinarily important because this is the point where the aesthetic joins the ethical."[63] It is important to notice this aspect to nurture elaborative empathy with marginalized subjectivities; this performance stages a useful scenario for thinking this through. Is the artist putting the audience in her shoes or, more precisely, inside what she feels regularly? Can the manipulation or the humiliation create awareness about how power is experienced by the non-powerful? Once care for the non-self is prioritized in the performance, there are many "others" to focus on and care for; empathic thought elaborates on this as well.

The practices of perceiving from a lower position of subjectivity, as subjects in a performance, and being perceived as perceiving, a metalevel of comprehension necessary for empathic thought, articulate an experience of empathic thought that mirrors double consciousness.[64] Double consciousness, then as today, speaks of the positionality of subjects. On the one hand, it could be said that representation here acts as an alibi to once again give white men what they want—a hypersexualized Latina body to play with. On the other hand, Nao's body is also a place where gay liberation grapples with forms of religion and sexual repression that "conquered" other nonconforming bodies—that is, "that mutilated, dismembered and exiled part of their world."[65] If this is the elaboration of a human and social body, which body is it? This performance shows that a body is construed, at least partly, in the eye of the beholder.

Intentions and free will are at play here in how we imagine other forms of life, and how we imagine we care, which is modeled by context. Categorization of identities might affect which concrete imaginations we come to the table with, and also what identities we can perceive. While the category of "Latina" was evident to most of the people to whom I showed this performance, the category of "queer Latina" was less evident. Perceiving both categories might "serve to orient imagination and memory towards one of the alternatives."[66] Some people perceived Nao to be experiencing feelings of empowerment and the pleasure of iconoclasm, so the emotion of empathy thrived in parallel emotions. For others, this "disrespect of religion" and the embrace of the spicy Latina paradigm prevented any empathy. The empowerment proposed by the performance could not be echoed because it seemed "infelicitous." So elaborative empathy relies on emotional memories that are both empathic and egoistic; egoistic means that the object of my concern falls outside the other person's feelings: for example, facing two person's fearful expressions, I echo their fear because I think I might be in danger as well. Literary works repeatedly present us with necessarily non-egoistic imaginations of emotion-rich situations. For the most part, we are engaged by the emotional interests of the characters. In this way, literature provides a remarkable source for affecting our inclinations toward empathy and our skills regarding empathy.[67] In performance, the author/persona can be affected directly by the audience's reactions, which often can be experienced together with the piece. This sets the conditions of possibility to incorporate multiple episodic memories at once and to understand that an emotion or situation that is not empowering for me might be empowering for Bustamante. Elaborative empathy pushes us to understand the conditions of possibility of this empowerment.

In a second-degree audience, empathic thought can disperse onto multiple subject positions or focus on one. Focusing on the feelings of a white participant would not be the same as focusing on the feelings of the performer wearing a harness with a phallic element (if that is our main perception) or the feelings of the performer being objectified (if that is our main perception) or the performer having a good time (if that is our main perception). One's empathy can focus on the feelings of the participant who appears to have a disability, or any other participant whose emotional well-being we were to attend the most.[68] Reactions to the performance would focus on some emotion that one of the participants is perceived to be feeling. Many explained empowerment as derived from the humiliation or submission of white men; other vantage points would empathize with penance through the feeling of humiliation or guilt, which is either enjoyed or not. Bustamante acknowledges that this was part of her intention:

I guess I was humiliating people when I look back at it. I guess my idea was to humiliate people in a comical way, and I didn't really give much thought to how people might feel about it. I just thought it would be funny.

Do you think they did feel humiliated?

The people who participated?

Yes.

Yes, I think they might have enjoyed the humiliation, but I think, maybe some people watching felt humiliated for them. I don't know.

Did you talk to them afterward?

No, it was a really big audience and the whole place was full, like three hundred people. It was very quick; I probably threw my clothes on and left.[69]

Some readings of the performance perceive the camaraderie and playfulness supposedly derived from acting together; yet others feel offended by the disrespect of religion or the objectification of the female body. Feeling offended might not obstruct empathy—for example, if it is overpowered by the feeling that the performer is making a mistake, or that something did not go according to script. Even when concentrating on bodies alone, experience and focus shift between white bodies, female bodies, queer bodies, disabled bodies, trans bodies, and bodies with many other identities, as does our initial assessment of how those selves are actually feeling. In many cases there will be a disconnection between how spectators feel the other must feel and how they perceive they are feeling.

Feminist film critics have used the concept of spectator to refer to the subject position constructed by the representation. The spectator here is not a real "person," but a viewing position "constructed by the signifying practice itself."[70] For Sawin, the subject positions enabled by culture and genre demand an understanding of both the actual and the constructed subject positions, but, most importantly, "we must recognize that these discursive positions in a sense 'create' the participants (as performer/spectator), while the participants (as performer/audience) reciprocally 'create' these positions as effective social realities by embodying and reinstating them."[71] Bustamante is acutely aware of the power of performance in creating these positions. Sometimes she promises the interactive nature of performance just to put the audience "on edge":

I do like kind of threaten interaction even if I don't use it. It does put people on the edge if they think they are going to be part of a performance. Even if I don't interact with people, I threaten them.
Besides alertness, what else do you expect to get out of it?
I think the people become more empathetic to the person I am interact-

ing with either because they are happy it's not them or they wish it were them. Puts the audience directly in a kind of role, in the way of the performance in a way, then they can see themselves inside the performance more clearly if you are looking at other people inside of it.[72]

This threat of interaction is one of the very essences of the power of performance, and even if perceived with a degree of separation—that is, from a second-degree audience—it adds another layer of situational knowledge to be empathic with: the person who is being "staged" or the audience member who is half theatrical prop and half actor. Because Sawin is referring to actual people who sit and watch, there is a third discursive position that is not fully acknowledged in her anthropological study. While the "nonparticipant" audience watching the performance filmed that day is largely a sonic presence of laughter and silence, the people watching the video in a classroom, at home, or in a library, though not producing the same "social realities," do embody a third level of discourse: discussion. When teachers/professors introduce videos or initiate discussions, there is a viewing position constructed, no matter how careful we are to provide diverse, multiple perspectives in the conversation. Previous material covered, the class title and description, the institution where we work, all our previous comments, our way of dressing and behaving, our tone, our style as educators, all those things and more build a spectator. In this realm, both virtual and physical audiences draw on past experiences that shape their viewing position.

I study Bustamante's 1992 performance as a way of thinking today, within the realm of contemporary problems, about the possibility of cultural understanding that goes together with the exploration of subaltern identities. I think it is important to keep in mind the psychic borderlands and the violence accompanying the contact zones that serve as the material reality for Moraga's and Spillers's theories. The epistemic conditions that the notion of flesh—a liberated subject position—promotes must be acknowledged to explore what routes of affective empathy this performance allows, and what its relation is to the present.[73] Bustamante posed *Indigurrito* as her contribution to the many performances that commemorated the five hundredth anniversary of the conquest of America. It was performed in May 1992 in San Francisco, and it promised to address with humor and sarcasm the issues that the five-hundred-year commemoration brought to collective attention.

During the protests that followed the killing of George Floyd, many monuments and murals have been removed or defaced, by force or by consent. Christopher Columbus figures prominently among the historical characters that have been deemed highly controversial, as this character is often invoked to celebrate the Italian American heritage by celebrating the Hispanic legacy of the conquest. With Columbus Day, the state gave these subjects who had been recently accepted into whiteness a piece of the past related to imperial power.[74] Questions around commemorations so well revisited in 1992 continue to be asked today, this time in regard to politics, the inclusion of minorities, and systemic racism within the United States. *Indigurrito* brings to the table the topics of symbolic violence and psychological violence by complicating demands to commemorate the Hispanic conquest.

The nexus between self and other locates a problem in the idea of flesh. While one might think that flesh, the concentration of ethnicity "taken for granted," poses a problem that is self-evident, that is not so once one tries to explain what desires are mobilized by the epistemic avenues set by people as audience and people as spectators (that is, as vantage points). The imagined problem constructs a viewing position. Sometimes the posed problem is not the one imagined—and sometimes it cannot be imagined.

In brief, it is crucial to acknowledge the way that categorizations influence attention, connection, and care. By looking at Bustamante's artistic choices, we can see her movement toward areas of power more in tune with kinship perceived and experienced as empowering. Analyzing the perspectives of different subject positions is a way of perceiving the possibility of different forms of experiencing or testing the experience of power. The role of the body informs "readings" of action in performance. Empathic thought that reaches out to imagine conditions of possibility and contexts of enunciation, whether verbal or physical, contributes to the experience of elaborative empathy. Spontaneous empathy demands little mobilization of ideas; elaborative empathy, instead, causes the individual to develop skills geared to understanding other selves that are not like "us." In enactments of power, the notion of a "minoritarian other" needs to grapple with notions of ethnicity surrounding the Latinx body. Performance constructs reciprocal positions for audience and performer in the classroom and in society. The desires that are mobilized obey not only personal preferences but also social sensibilities. These social sensibilities are part of history, for as we can see through Bustamante's viewpoints, one cannot disregard the special universe that was San Francisco in 1992. Once one attends to the investment in gendered subjective positions studied by Sawin, one can see that *Indigurrito* employs a phallic food object to recreate *another* type of investment. Acknowledging the dissimilar consequences of similar actions opens the door for empowerment to be conceptualized in more than one way, especially in regard to subjects whose flesh is often recruited in reenactments of difference. There is a need to go beyond spontaneous empathy to understand with what we are sympathizing. First, there is a connection—sympathy—and then this connection needs to be critically examined through the inclusion of other, less powerful subject positions within our personal space of concern.

2

Empathy and Puzzlement

"La gente que vio 'Dominicanish,' si creyeron que eso era Josefina Báez, se jodieron." (Those who saw 'Dominicanish' and thought that was Josefina Baez, got screwed, fooled.)

THE PURPOSE OF THIS CHAPTER is to explore how emotional memories and puzzlement interact in empathic thought and what role they play in fostering elaborative empathy. *Dominicanish* (1999) by Josefina Báez is presented as a performance that creates the conditions of possibility for puzzlement. As an enactment of power, *Dominicanish* deals with emotions very different from those inspired by Nao Bustamante's *Indigurrito*. The relationship posited between self and other is one in which the other is off-stage to begin with, but also one in which the artist/author creates a space for the self apart from stereotypes surrounding identitarian categories such as the Latina or the Black woman. *Dominicanish* presents multiple selves, all belonging to the performer, as a way to shift expectations, stereotypes, and discourse. No participatory game is employed to attract the audience's attention.

This presentation of the self relates to the notion of occurrence employed by Odette Casamayor-Cisneros to study Afro-Cuban visual artists. Instead of confronting stereotypical valuations (and devaluations) of Afro-Latinos, occurrence "locates" subjects in a manner that "represents the experience of being black without conceiving blackness as otherness. Occurrence allows thinking of blackness beyond otherness."[1] As Casamayor-Cisneros explains, "Here, blackness is not shouted. . . . Rather, blackness simply occurs. When one passes from an aesthetic of confrontation to one of occurrence, critical discourse shifts from the art object to the spectator."[2] This resonates with certain aspects of José Esteban Muñoz's notion of disidentification, which is discussed later in the chapter, for occurrence disidentifies as a way of going beyond notions of otherness, thus reclaiming the prerogatives assigned to the official self—among them, the lack of need for self-explanation or self-identification. Both *Indigurrito* and *Dominicanish* challenge the expectations of identity performance, the former by means of a confrontation, the latter through occurrence.

This notion of occurrence also bears some similarities to Black feminism, as articulated by Patricia Hill Collins. One could say that Báez puts in motion one of Black feminism's basic themes: self-definition and self-valuation. Self-definition challenges the validation process that imposes stereotypical images, thus rejecting harmful images; self-valuation "replaces externally derived images," thus producing constructive and accurate images of the self.[3] In her sociological study, Collins wanted to show the usefulness of identifying and using one's own standpoint when conducting research. In *Dominicanish*, Báez follows this theme when she "challenges stereotypical images of Afro-American [and Afro-Dominican] womanhood" and therefore "values her own consciousness from a self-defined standpoint."[4] This self-constructed standpoint releases the viewer from the usual images that define *afrolatinidad* and also disassembles dualistic thinking about identity. Collins's notions of self-definition and self-valuation value the status of the outsider within and offer tools to break with dualistic forms of oppression. Her essay posits that these tools were derived from knowledge and skills that Black women's position in society most likely had already gained for them. Both self-definition and

FIGURE 2.1 Josefina Baez performing *Dominicanish*, a performance piece informed by many sources, including Indian dance and quotidian hand usage. Photo by Luisa Sanchez for Ay Ombe Theatre, 2002.

self-valuation insist on restructuring the subjects' power: one does it by taking control of the mechanisms of the definition, while the other does it by addressing its contents. Self-definition also rejects internally imposed images, so it is not a question of inside/outside, but of process/content. Lorgia García Peña notes that "Josefina Báez' 'Dominicanish' is a speech act that demands space for her art."[5] This space goes way beyond the verbal register and a traditional linear realist approach, approximating the experience of migration in a "self reflective play with genre—dance, poetry, performance—and a constant fluid movement between cultures" that enables Baez to express a radical and open conception of *dominicanidad*.[6] Importantly, the performance does not announce her self-valuation; instead, the performance simply occurs.

The Black Dominican body is not, of course, interchangeable with the African American body, but as García Peña proposes in *Translating Blackness*, "for Black Latinxs, translating their racialized immigrant Latinx exclusion by aligning with US Black historical experiences can help them become legible to the nation, access resources, and build antiracist and anticolonial solidarity."[7] Up until now studies on Afrolatinos have been concerned with the problem of visibility; for a long time this group was "lost among the predominant classifications," or as Ana Maurine Lara noted, this group struggled to be seen.[8] Yet, once seen, a narrow emphasis on the differences can leave out of frame "the convergences of colonialism, immigration, and blackness that shape Black Latinx lives in diaspora."[9] García Peña seems to have stepped beyond the problem of visibility to pose the struggle in terms of translation. Translation implies a need for legibility and understanding, which she addresses through the concept of vaivén and its "dynamic possibilities: to be coming and going to and from the nation and hegemonic notions of belonging is to challenge the social order, the structure of the market and the ideologies of national identifications."[10] In *Dominicanish*, to challenge stereotypical images of Afro-American and Afro-Dominican womanhood means to inhabit mobile experiences of belonging and unbelonging.

Performance

> Josefina Baez' *Dominicanish* (November 6–8), which explores the Dominican experience in America, will be the center's theater offering. Playwright Baez will appear in the piece that will be directed by Claudio Mir and will feature trumpeter Ross Huff.[11]

Dominicanish was first performed in November 1999 at Dance Theater Workshop in New York; its final performance was ten years later at Harlem Stage in November 2009. During those ten years, the piece was performed innumerable times around the world, including in New Zealand, Peru, Australia, and Finland. The performance begins with a film clip of Dominican-Haitian dancers dancing to the rhythm of Gaga (or rara); this is a Gaga from the Batey (a sugarcane workers' town or municipal district) La Ceja, a Batey from La Romana, where Báez is from.[12] As it ends, a person enters the stage playing the saxophone, and minutes later Báez appears behind him, moving toward the center of the stage while performing dance movements in slow motion. During the first three performances a saxophone was employed, but all following performances used trumpets instead. Báez says that the trumpet is her favorite instrument; its sound feels like home. As later becomes apparent, the dance movements belong to an Indian dance, a southern Indian dance tradition called Kuchipudi. Right from the start, the film, music, and dance are prone to puzzle the audience.[13] As the performance advances, it moves from the Indian dance to struggles with language, then to the use of common slogans. Báez refers to the difficulties of learning English and succeeds in imitating different accents, moving with ease between a marked and an unmarked accent, between Spanish and English, and between different intonations, speeds, and volumes of speech.[14] Speech, pronunciation exercises, and soundscape swirl together pivoting from phonological and lexical transferences. There is a corpus of phrases that represent the voices of the nonimmigrant Dominicans to capture Báez's experience of being treated as a tourist or an outsider in her home, while at the same sounding as a grammar lesson in the return visit scenario.[15] Many critics have focused on the pronunciation aspects in these scenes. For Stevens, "[t]he multiplicity of linguistic registers—ranging from public service announcements, the voices of teenagers and vendors, song lyrics, language lessons, acronyms, snippets from tales from *Panchatantra*—keep the non-Aristotelian structure of the narrative flowing from one story to the next."[16] I argue that this multiplicity of registers also invites a reading that falls outside the binary Spanish /English, to avoid constituting Spanish and/or accented pronunciation as the privileged element of a cultural "Latina-ness."

The performance affirms Báez's cultural heritage at various moments, such as when she talks about the *discos del alma con afro* and the Isley Brothers. At some point, Báez reaffirms her African heritage by announcing, "Black is beautiful" and uttering other slogans from the Black Power movement of the 1960s. She also acknowledges the prevalent racism in Dominican history when she declares, "Balaguer, leave us alone." *Dominicanish* defies both US and Dominican racism.[17] Critics, such as Liamar Durán Almarza, Lorgia García Peña, and Roberto Irizarry, have noted that in affirming her African heritage, Báez subverts the Dominican myth of Haitian Blackness, which reads: if it's Black, it's Haitian, not Dominican. Unfortunately, this racist state was not a distant past, neither in the DR nor in the US. In November of 1994, twenty thousand Haitians were expelled at gunpoint from the Dominican Republic, leading to protests at the Dominican consulate in New York. Subsequent reforms to the constitution were made targeting Dominicans of Haitian descent. In 2013, a high court ruling in the Dominican Republic denaturalized those of Haitian heritage born in the DR, that denaturalization applied retroactively to 1929.[18] The last video of the performance is about the riots in Washington Heights and protests in response to the killing of Kiko García in 1992.

In *Dominicanish* there is an Afrolatina body performing Indian dances dressed in "an austere black cocktail dress, combined with a white pearl necklace and black low-heeled shoes. . . . The black attire of the performer visually evokes the aesthetics of female soul and jazz singers of the 1960s, particularly those of Billie Holiday," but even those who miss the cultural reference can notice that the attire helps the performer defy various forms of exoticization or ethnification.[19] The same happens with the Indian dance: most would catch its Indian origin, few the specific part of India, but nearly all will find that the dance contributes to an identity that, as García Peña states, "seems, in the Dominican context, strange and out of place."[20] The performance shifts the ground you think you're standing on; if you don't know that Black people are called *indios* in the Dominican Republic, you will not find ironic the lexical transference the dance plays with.[21] This is also the case for other personal experiences of struggle, discrimination, and oppression the audience could perceive.

Dominicanish originated as a performance of gratitude. Báez comments that she trained in Indian dances, "as a devotee," initially for "other reasons than performance." Later on, "I had a surgery in both knees, and I thought that I was not going to walk, so then after that, I started dancing and creating out of . . . homage . . . out of gratitude. It is a performance of gratitude; it's love."[22]

One line that deals with the struggle of learning English—"Yo no voy a poner la boca así como un guante" (I'm not going to move my mouth like a glove)—presents an emotional memory that relates to uneasy encounters with foreign languages and cultures. In this section, the performer explores a rejection of the unknown language and discomfort with the phonological demands it entails. We realize, though, that she learned English anyway. The performer moves easily between two languages, which was something many found reassuring, as it reaffirmed two or more identity positions. In this realm, we could say that it presents the possibility of feeling "differently." This appears to be a desired response, since Báez's own website, and some editions of the script, display this statement by Silvio Torres-Saillant: "One of the most important interventions that, to my knowledge, reflects on the Dominican cultural experience, we owe it to Josefina Báez, a New York-based performance artist, with her piece Dominicanish." Emotional memories are part of the Dominican cultural experience in the US.

Báez can be understood as fully debunking narrow views about blackness and latinidad. Báez not only performs but also produces facts and theories about the very notion of *experience*. "'Dominicanish' offers an open ontological framework where everything that empirically fits in the lives of the Dominican diaspora is part of the identity formation of what we are as a nation, here and there."[23] One year before *Dominicanish* was first performed, Torres-Saillant had called for something like that in one of his seminal essays, "The Tribulations of Blackness: Stages in Dominican Racial Identity": "I propose to avoid the pitfalls of investigating Dominican attitudes about race exclusively through the utterances of the ruling class by making an effort to assemble instances of active participation of Afro-Dominicans in building and defining their history. These instances, compiled from the field of social action, offer an invaluable living text, an indispensable document that could scarcely be produced by archival research alone."[24]

Báez's approach is much like that of Adrian Piper, another New York–based performer, who had ten years earlier also investigated attitudes about race in New York. Both are highly invested in the ontological aspects that Torres-Saillant underscores, identifying their own standpoints through an autobiographical enactment of power. Yet *Dominicanish* does not confront the viewer with its self-valuation and self-identification, at least not as overtly as Piper's *Cornered*, which confronts the viewer with the thesis that Black identity extends beyond visibility and that racial identity is a choice. The argument is meaningful to Piper because, as a biracial person, she is often read as white. "Passing" is hurtful for her in the situations in which racist comments are made in her presence. *Cornered* consists of a video recording played on a monitor installed in a corner inside a gallery. When it was on display at UCLA's Hammer Museum in 2014, at least one reviewer had an emotional response: "The video gives the feel that Piper is trying to establish herself as superior to the viewer and is obligated to educate them in their personal heritage, openly belittling the viewer."[25] Whether or not the video actually belittles the viewer is less important for my purposes than the way the installation creates subject positions in the audience.

Báez allows more flexibility for the audience, yet she shares with Piper a profound interest in using her own subject position to create art while doing research. In fact, in 1991 Piper became the first female African American philosophy professor to receive academic tenure in the United States.[26] Prior to *Cornered*, Piper focused on how artwork acts as a catalytic agent to promote change in the viewer without undergoing any permanent change itself.[27] Another system of knowledge is facilitated once alternative enactments of power grasp "form" as a catalytic agent. The fact that this change can occur is not surprising; by now, it has been occurring for ages. Collins asserts, "If Black women use their daily resources to be self-defined and self-valuating and to encourage others to reject objectification, then Black women's everyday behavior itself is a form of activism."[28] Patricia Hill Collins, however, is analyzing Black women's outsider status in academia. Báez's framework is within performance as social and artistic interaction.

Báez's Space

Dominicanish understands the expectation of thinking in dualities—dualities that, according to bell hooks, structure the ideological

FIGURE 2.2 Artist performing *Dominicanish*. Photo by Luisa Sanchez for Ay Ombe Theatre, 2002.

systems of domination in Western societies.[29] In the performance, Báez breaks with dualities by appealing to mismatched images and behaviors. There is a sustained tension between body language and verbal language that is never resolved nor explained: "Tension between what is said and what is danced? Yes, that is part of it, but not as an intention, when you work with the intensity of the body, there is always this tension and you have to feel it. That push and pull, that will give organicity."[30] Báez plays with expectations by subverting and opening new spaces of signification: the performance entails the presentation of a subject who prefers not to represent.

In *Dominicanish*, Báez employed a performative discourse that at that time was nowhere to be seen in anthologies by Latinos or Dominicans. "Báez was one of the pioneers of literature and theater focused on the experience of Dominican immigrants in the United States, especially in the New York area."[31] Part of this experience relates to "claiming and being claimed by two nation-states"; "suspended between the homeland and the host land."[32] "Yo soy el nie"

(I am the neither/nor), Báez affirms. Establishing a contrast with García Peña, who envisions this in-between-space as mainly uncomfortable owing to the "dual marginality" Dominican migrants face at home and abroad, Stevens chooses to highlight it to value its contribution to the creative act of homemaking.[33] While García Peña has also underscored the generative space of this state of neither/nor, most recently in *Translating Blackness*, it is important to notice that for Black Dominicans this "claiming and being claimed by two nation-states" works differently than for white Dominicans. That is, once the main elements informing the tension in the immigrant experience go from two nation-states to two identity categorizations, the experience of the push and pull, the neither/nor, the nepantla, might feel different because the dynamics of inclusion/exclusion change. In ways similar to Gloria Anzaldúa and the Nuyoricans' works, code switching integrates the language of *Dominicanish* as a way of breaking both Spanish and English syntaxes. Yet code-switching is only a small part of her discourse. Her performative language, as with her conception of research, is based on the care of the self:

> I train my performers to be in with no floor, to make the best decision from where they are, not where they wish . . . . So, then, taking care of the body, taking care of the thoughts, taking care of what you see, what you eat, what you listen.
>
> I don't have much to teach, but I am very good at reminding people that there is something before, during, and after. It is a whole system that I have based on very concrete stuff beyond spiritualism and god knows what. Something that I have tried since 1986, and people gets the results of it. It is very cool.

Báez established the Ay Ombe Theater Troupe in 1986. As a founder and director of Ay Ombe Theatre, she dedicated her efforts to "creative processes based on the autobiography and wellness of the doer;" she named this approach Performance Autology.[34] Her theater school and retreat receive all sorts of personal projects, such as theater performance pieces, dissertations, and personal works on a particular virtue.[35] In 2009, for example, she organized a theater retreat in India. She says that she founded the theater school she would have wanted to attend but could not find.[36]

Báez's conception of performance art training encompasses, first and foremost, the care of the mind aiming for beauty and happiness. In fact, at the end of each annual retreat, projects are evaluated according to their level of happiness. This conception of happiness is in tune with that of the Enlightenment philosopher Baruch Spinoza, who considered happiness to be that which strengthens conscience. Báez's activities and public lectures in the fields of literature and performance are part of the same personal research project: "[M]y research is about everything, or the best results of what I have done in life in physical, mental and spiritual terms."[37] Emotional memories are staged following her particular performative language: "Escuchamos [las] frases [de los textos creados] y vemos las imágenes que nos sugieren, en boca y cuerpo de otros. Porque al final, lo que vive uno lo vivimos todos" (We listen to the created works' sentences, and we see the images that these suggest, in the mouths and bodies of others. Because, in the end, what one lives, we all live).[38] This interest propels the collective work that the company generates. A member of the company clarifies, "La pieza es un relato que no se centra en acontecimientos o hechos, sino en el impacto emocional que han tenido los hechos de su vida en la protagonista" (The piece is a story that is not centered around events or facts, but rather on the emotional impact that life events have had on the protagonist's life).[39] For Báez,

> Before the emotion is felt, it is a thought, it is a memory, it is a lot of stuff, in fact . . . it comes from different sources, so then depends . . . both where is coming from, and where it is going to land, and it is getting created as emotion in this body, and when I say body, I have in mind the emotional body, the thought body, the heart body, every single aspect of bodies that you would like to mention. So, then, if we are . . . to know beyond fact, it is wisdom . . . that we live in a very mobile terrain, that everything is changing. If we know that as a fact, we are able to understand and dance with every single freaking emotion that comes. So, we won't bend out of shape.[40]

The demand for a space for her art that García Peña underlines calls for bodies of knowledge to be staged. These bodies of knowledge achieve poignant literalness when preserving the spaces of memory and preserving the body are part of a common emotional memory. "[F]or a long time communities of color have had 'to carry around knowledge and stories in our bodies,' because resources were not devoted to preserving the spaces that held those stories," asserts the poet Elizabeth Alexander.[41] In the Dominican Republic, the preservation of the spaces of communities of color runs against the notion of national space, which structures itself as the space of that which is not Black. Báez herself often declares that "two amazing things have created me: exclusion and invisibility. Those two things are amazing to me, because I created a whole fucking system to take care of myself"; "[or better said], what have been important, or what have informed my existence have been exclusion and invisibility. This is very fucking big, that with that I have created this woman that you see now, this woman, the performer."[42] It is indeed amazing how out of invisibility and exclusion—sentiments that are neither refreshing nor uplifting (once one takes the abstract aroma away from them)—Báez created a creative, loving safe artistic space. The very fucking *big thing*, I believe, has nothing to do with the alibi that claims, "you see? With determination, everybody can." It relates, instead, to a recent comment from a colleague: "Amazing, no? That we still manage to go on living and even preserve our mental health!" When García Peña poses that Black Latinidad as an epistemology is a way of understanding and producing knowledge from the site of unbelonging, we can appreciate how this resonates with Báez's insight on how exclusion and invisibility informed her existence.[43]

We can see how crucial elements of Báez's vision of performance (and school of theater) are already present in *Dominicanish*. The visual aspect of emotional memories creates another dynamic of power for the empathic subject to relate to. Báez encourages an empathy in which you accompany another's emotions rather than being swept away by them. For her, such engagement preserves the self from being crushed under the burden of empathy. She explains, "My chosen responsibility is to accompany my tribe, people in my tribe and at large too."[44] The empathic subject in the audience would have to dwell in another's place, a place built by disidentifying stereotypical images from the common landscapes of identity. The enactment of power functions through the particular disidentificatory features of the artist as artwork. One can empathize with what she is "not" doing. For subjects who see her as a member of an out-group, this defines another way of thinking about the other, but for many placed on the outskirts of identitarian categories, this performance provides another way of working with the "self."

Emotional memories are affected by critical-period experiences, a term used to refer to an infant's process of learning how to feel. These experiences affect our inclination to empathize, in part because they provide initial rehearsals of attending to the emotional expression of others.[45] The Nuyorican poet and professor Miguel Algarín refers concretely to this phenomenon in *Survival: Supervivencia*: "When I was a child, I trusted my mother completely. Whenever she felt safe, I felt safe. I remember looking out for my mother's signals. I was always alert for signals of fear."[46] These experiences set up mimetic empathic responses that could be restricted to family members or identity groups. We can take, for example, the case of writer and poet Piri Thomas, an Afro–Puerto Rican whose critical experiences taught him that the Black identity was not an in-group identity, and most importantly, that feeling Black was a dysphoric experience even in the very same family he belonged to. Maybe Báez, as José Esteban Muñoz describes in "Stages: Queers, Punks, and the Utopian Performative," is prompting the viewer to feel, yes, but to feel in a different, more critical way, questioning those automatic, reactive emotions ingrained in us by society, to reach out with openness and curiosity to other's feelings, to truly *understand* not just the other's feelings, but the how and why of them as well; "Instead of saying I understand, or I am here with you, feel it: ¿Qué te hace sentir esto? [what makes you feel that way?]."[47]

I agree with García Peña and Durán Almarza that *Dominicanish* exercises resistance, but from a point of view emphasizing empathic thought, what stands out is the artist's body as artwork that simply "occurs," beyond confrontation. Both in New York and in the Dominican Republic, cultural systems demand conformity to mainstream identities. For Durán Almarza, the fact that the protagonist adopts "a position of resistance to both Dominican and New York cultural systems" problematizes identitarian demands.[48] If we shift our focus from Báez as protagonist of the play to Báez as author and intellectual, we see more than resistance. Given our interest in empathic thought, the Brechtian strategy that García Peña identifies in the monologue's opening minutes as a performance of language can be extrapolated to other languages in this performance—not because they are in themselves "producing feelings of confusion and anxiety," but because as much as "the audience seems puzzled yet interested in what this mouth is molding as it produces these unfamiliar sounds," the same happens with the South Indian Kuchipudi dance moves.[49] This extrapolation might even respond to Brecht's distrust of the manipulative uses of empathy in theater. Alberta Szalita notes that Bertold Brecht became convinced that theater had to be liberated from empathy and catharsis.[50] Here, elaborative empathy and its relation to performance further complicate this occluded relationship to reopen the stage to the thought of emotions. García Peña herself notes that "Báez's corporeal language seems to contradict her speech," and "Báez's performance succeeds in proposing multiplicity as a more genuine and realistic idea of identity."[51] Not many are aware of a history that connects an Indian dance and the Dominican Republic: "In the 1800s thousands of East Indians were brought to the Caribbean as indentured servants."[52] This "most realistic idea of identity" not only challenges preconceptions, it also assigns more effort to empathic emotional memories. As emotional memories are activated in the elaborative empathy process, it forces viewers to reflect on the self. Puzzlement acts in this performance as a second timing, in which prefabricated tandems between identities and problems do not hold. Puzzlement helps to step away from a notion of an "other" that is so self-evident that it becomes transparent.

Puzzlement, Empathy and Emotional Memories

Puzzlement plays a role in the link between emotional memories and empathy. It attends to the unknown in a way that rejects both the impossibility of knowing (being familiar with) and an unproblematized familiarity with experiences of disenfranchisement outside our way of life. An unproblematized being-familiar-with renders positions of privilege as relative, minimizing their influence on our perception. Puzzlement as a response to the emotional memories staged by Josefina Báez is a much-welcomed element in the empathic process that results from the artist's deliberate disidentification with current expectations (explaining the self to be data graspable, collectible). In one of the performances in New Zealand, a white woman shared that "my family were settlers, but I felt that I was the migrant, for the first twenty minutes, we wanted to get to the performance with you, and you would take us and leave us, it was very uncomfortable." Báez was delighted. She was like, "Oh, my god! Wonderful, yeah! This is the way we feel, not in the *performance* . . . *in life*! As a migrant, so you . . . what she shared was *beyond definition . . . the feeling of it*, the emotion of it!"[53] It is very refreshing that Báez does not explain to her audience what the performance is about, but it can at the same time generate unease.

Puzzlement is not the same as confusion, but it encompasses confusion, especially in efforts geared toward encouraging empathic thought in the classroom. In *The Spark of Learning*, Sarah Cavanaugh points out that a curiosity-invoking frame of mind can be generated by confusion. For her, curiosity and confusion "can be considered dark mirrors of each other."[54] She remarks that while curiosity is considered a positive emotion—her book is about emotions in the college classroom—confusion is often considered a negative emotion.[55] In our educational system, confusion is deemed a sign that something is not working, but at times, its lack can be more indicative of dysfunctionality than its presence. There is an aversion to confusing the student, and likewise, the teaching methods of professors who present materials causing confusion are deemed defective. Like a fire, confusion has to be put out as quickly as possible. Many times, "I am confused" means "tell me what I need to think or know so that I can repeat it back to you later," but other times it doesn't, and those are the most precious moments that can truly spark the learning process. Both confusion and puzzlement draw attention to a gap between a state of knowledge and what is perceived as knowable.[56] Drawing on Ian Leslie's work, Cavanaugh distinguishes between puzzles and mysteries. It is here that we can rearticulate the power of a curiosity-invoking frame in the realm of empathy. For Leslie, puzzles open a knowledge gap with a definite solution, while mysteries have more complex and nuanced solutions that might forever elude solution.[57] Understanding people is not like understanding theorems. If academic knowledge of out-group others in our America makes it seem as if we can use a formula to understand other people, there is a problem.[58] Conversely, if others are presented as unknowable, there is a problem as well.

To consider the role of puzzlement in emphatic thought efforts, I take two elements from Leslie's work: the perceived knowledge gap of puzzles and the effortful and sustained acts of epistemic curiosity required by mysteries. In short, the gap and the quest—the curiosity and the drive—are crucial. An interest in empathy as a process rather than as a result is key for exploring relationships between groups in the cases where in-group/out-group relations are staged. This is so because gaining skills in elaborative empathy, taking empathy as an effortful process, assures the attainment of knowledge that is flexible and can adapt to perception. Not all out-group others will be the same. Not all identities encounter the same problems, nor do people perceive and feel experiences in the same manner.

Cavanaugh cites Beckes, Coan, and Hasselno's study in which friends feel the same way toward a threat to the self as they do toward a threat to a close friend; the closer the self-reported overlap in self-identity, the stronger the correlation.[59] Hogan also describes the predisposition to empathy based on overlapping identities in *What Literature Can Teach Us about Emotions.* So, how do we train ourselves to respond to other people's experiences in kind, if not to the same degree, when we do not identify ourselves with the other person in the same manner, or when there is a puzzling gap between what we know and what we expect?

Elaborative empathy involves openness to parallel emotional experience and skills at understanding another person's emotions, such as attending (attention), simulating (imagination), modeling (perception), and categorizing, which we discussed in the previous chapter. Modeling benefits from a wealth of prior emotional episodes that might serve as models, but what happens when there is not a great wealth of emotional episodes or those are insufficient to model out-group emotional experience?[60] Hogan posits that literature presents students with a source for developing empathic inclinations. This is particularly true for literary works that explain and describe the feelings that emerge in particular situations. Yet performance art sometimes exhibits a reluctance to explain and describe—this reluctance is clear in *Dominicanish*. Does that mean that these performances cannot be a source for developing empathic inclinations and skills?

Usually, the activation of emotional memories responds to a perceived parallel between the present eliciting conditions and the past experience.[61] For example, I see somebody is afraid and I remember a moment when I was afraid, or, more precisely, how that felt. With *Dominicanish*, the parallel might be easily established at the linguistic level—that is, through the feelings of frustration and resistance expressed verbally in its monologues. Emotional congruence might also be established at the level of bodily experience, such as the awkwardness of moving the mouth in an unknown position to pronounce a word and the sense of effort required. Identifying past memories of frustration or resistance can generate emotional congruence that informs elaborative empathy.

But what happens when emotional memories do not bring the self to a similar past situation? What happens when the situation cannot be identified? I propose that this puzzlement can still enable elaborative empathy. Parallels—for instance, memories of the same place or memories of the same people—could be retrieved while watching *Dominicanish*, but, interestingly, they might not; this does not necessarily constitute an obstacle for elaborative empathy.[62] In fact, a reactive association of identities and problems commonly demotivates the search for other systems of knowledge, identifying a problem without bothering to learn about *other's* problems.[63] A hyperbolic sketch of this elaborative empathy obstructed by the automatic association of an identity with a problem would look like this: Since I know your identity category, the tag that society assigns to you, I already know your problems. I do not need to listen (or read) to what you are telling me; I really have nothing to learn. Again, this is a sketch, but I observe this frame of mind regularly. And the question that this situation begs is "How do I learn about a problem I do not know about?"

Báez explains the importance of memory in her performances: "In my work, you can say that memory is at the backbone. I consider myself master of memories." Usually, she continues, "I am playing with a memory that I bring to the present, and it is extended to the future. And so, the memory is the base, but at times, it is there intertwined with the three tenses."[64] The puzzlement induced by *Dominicanish*, the meaning that cannot be explained, the causal explanation not yet identified, works precisely on that which goes contrary to expectations and that changes according to perception. Different spectators will perceive different gaps, yet all experience the tensions explored between verbal language and body language that are prone to causing puzzlement in those exposed to mainstream, hegemonic notions of identities that are not their own. Báez is explicit about her reluctance to "confound" for the sake of it; rather, this nonlinear, nonexplanatory narrative is what she has to offer. If there is any intention at all, the goal is to create a state of high alertness.[65] Self and other construct the terms of engagement, but in this performance, emotional memories function fluidly. The emphasis is on the negative space of cognition, in a disidentificatory manner: The focus is on that which falls outside parallel emotions and memorable situations—that is, puzzlement.

Báez's play about Dominican identity explores confusing perceptions and their connections to emotional memories.

These memories can be empathic or egoistic, depending on whether we can remember emotional episodes in which we care for the feelings of others or ourselves. Derek Matravers points out that it is easier to bridge the gap between the empathizer and the target if the former has had the same experience as the latter, but what happens if this is not the case? Matravers shares my concern with an apparently overdetermined optimism regarding the conditions of possibility for empathy:

> Partly because we are trying to replicate what it is like to be in some emotional state, there are many ways in which attempts at empathy can fail. We might lack information about the target's situation or we might lack a grasp of what, in this situation, is salient to them. We might misconstrue their character, or it might simply be that our imagined inputs do not have the same causal ramifications in our mental economy as their actual inputs have in theirs. Emotional states are notoriously sensitive to details, and a salient detail from the target's perspective might simply be something that either cannot or does not register from the empathizer's perspective.[66]

The possibility of attention without the retrieval of parallel memories opens a vast array of avenues for empathy training. Yet they are extremely effortful. "The effortful nature of elaborative empathy suggests the possibility that we may be more or less motivated to engage in such a process, and that we might be more or less skilled at it."[67] In the environment of the academic classroom in the US educational system where students are conceived as clients, "and the client is always right," motivation and skills need to be considered with this in mind. That is, in the US, where most of the students are treated as clients and inhabit a culture of branding that sells an identity with every consumer choice made, how identities are perceived is highly curated. People (not only students) enjoy feeling "empathic," but the effortful acquisition of skills in something like "empathy" (that is not yet? monetized, does not center around personal profit) is a complex task.[68] Puzzlement can present an occasion to step out of the manicured experience and explore personal thoughts.

Emotional memories—like skill memories, such as how to ride a bike—are "implicit" memories. Thus, when activated, they do not lead us to think about some representational content. When we activate the skill of riding a bike, we do not represent the processes to ourselves. Rather, we just ride the bike.[69] Common attachment patterns, based on our previous practices, influence our contextualization of people and categories, which is what we call identity categories. Although we might think objective observations cause the release of emotions and emotions materialize, it is to a large extent a matter of what we have practiced before. The way in which we integrate perception and memory is guided by our working memory— that is, inferential routines that identify objects, infer causes, and construct anticipations.[70] A reflective take on empathy calls for identifying our inferential routines and examining them more closely.

To finish this section, I want to return to Susan Lanzoni's take on empathy as "a tool, a technique, a practice and an aspiration."[71] None of those attributes would be grasped in the classroom by taking lecture notes. "Empathy links us to other beings," but the nature of the link, and the emotional memories required to establish it, matter.[72] Szalita views empathy as one of the important "mechanisms by which we bridge the gap between experience and thought."[73] An important and often overlooked aspect of this mechanism is that a gap has to become evident. Disidentity and disidentifications, which we will discuss in the next section, open this gap and work with it, "shuffling back and forth between reception and production."[74] Muñoz thinks of disidentification as both a hermeneutical performance and a possibility for freedom.[75] Both the stylistics of the self and elaborative empathy cultivate a part of oneself that transcends the self. While for Muñoz, disidentification is a strategy called on by minoritarian subjects, it can, and at times should, be called on to empathically detach oneself from conflations of experience and thought that keep the gap of elaborative empathy shut. In an era so absorbed with the production of a self to trade with, this *impersonal dimension* that goes beyond one's present self rehearses possible future relations of power that allow *another self* to be realized.

Disidentification and Empathy

The notion of disidentification revisits the alternatives of confrontation and occurrence detailed by Casamayor-Cisneros and of self-identification and self-valuation described by Collins. Muñoz reenvisions Michel Pêcheux's disidentification to move outside of Althusser's structure of interpellation and into the terrain of queer performativity.[76] For Muñoz, disidentification is a survival strategy employed by a minority spectator to resist and *confound* socially prescriptive patterns of identification.[77] Muñoz does not analyze *Dominicanish*, but this performance certainly does "confound socially prescriptive patterns."[78] Báez enters the performance art's representational economy on her own terms, embracing what Pêcheux calls "a non-subjective position."[79] Her take on the notion of audience gives her ample artistic and personal liberty,

> I respect my audience so much that I don't have to worry about them. You know, they would like it or they won't like it. That it is all right. Because I am an audience myself and this is the way I like to be treated. I am a very responsible audience. I am a very responsible reader, so then my audience would not dictate how I have to do because then I am cheating myself and I am cheating them. What I have to do is genuine work, this is my task, and my audience would do whatever they want.[80]

She exercises control over her form of representation when, for example, she founds the theater school she would have liked to attend. Likewise, she treats the audience as she would herself expect to be treated. Developed in response to Althusser's considerations of ideology, Pêcheux's theory adds a crucial consideration of "historical devices of experimentation-transformation."[81] Much like Judith Butler, Pêcheux wanted to think about an option to interpellation that is neither oppositional nor uncritical, a third option. Given that we cannot extricate ourselves from ideology (and the subject form), Pêcheux thought of disidentification as the effect of overthrowing-rearranging the complex of ideological (and discursive) formations, transforming rather than abolishing predominant subject-forms.[82] In creating a new school of theater, a field that is itself concerned with the performance of subjectivities, Báez is doing just that. The way in which *Dominicanish* rearranges multiple linguistic registers and genre speaks of transformation and disidentification.

Muñoz's *Disidentifications* engaged with the possibilities offered by Pêcheux's notion of disidentification, especially with the possibility of this "ideology in reverse that works on and against itself," by presenting concrete instances.[83] Using specific examples and deliberately emphasizing race and gender further complicates subjective identity relations. An intersectional approach to the relationship between self and others transforms not only the reception of mainstream "interpellations" but also the production of minoritarian hermeneutics. Disidentification, for Muñoz, goes one step beyond exposing what is taken for granted as paradigmatic by representing a "disempowered politics or positionality that has been rendered unthinkable by the dominant culture."[84] Josefina Báez's Afro-Latina, Afro-Dominican identity has been rendered unthinkable by racist policies destined to structure Dominican national ideology as non-Black, but also by the pressure to choose either the Latino or the Black community as a place to localize practices of belonging. Representing the unthinkable can lead to puzzlement.

García Peña notes that Báez openly challenges Dominican and American discourses on race when she decodes monolithic ideas of race and ethnicity and reappropriates the power of self-identification.[85] And Báez leaves no doubt about it when she comments on the events surrounding Black Lives Matter protests,

A mí me parece que estamos en un momento en que por lo menos está visible que la diferencia es una jodienda, y ahora estamos ahí ...extermination... exclusion scapegoat.... Hay una historia muy jodida, pero para mí lo más importante es que es ...

It seems to me that we are in a moment when at least it is visible that the difference is screwing us and now we are there ... extermination... exclusion *scapegoat*... There is a very fucked-up story, but for me the most important thing is that it is ... what is vital right now, what is vital right now, is fucking respect. We ought to respect the lives of others.[86]

Both García Peña and Durán Almarza cite the part of *Dominican-ish* in which Báez affirms, "Black is beautiful, black is my color," but the performance's less interpellative moments, in my opinion, have a stronger disidentificatory effect. For Durán Almarza, the resistance to Dominican and American identitarian demands springs from a particular interstitial location, the Dominican York community. Báez told me she was one of the first artists to self-define this way. She explained that the term began to be used in the seventies by the radio announcer Frank Krawinkel, who used it to refer to five basketball players living in New York and playing in the Dominican Republic. One of these players was Báez's brother, Hector. In the eighties, the term acquired pejorative tones in its use to stereotype Dominicans as violent drug dealers. It is in this climate that Báez uses it for the first time in an interview in the DR, not to break the stereotype from within, which she might have afterward, but because she liked the rhythm of the phrase and the pleasure of having defined in one single phrase her two countries.[87] While the power of relocating the self is undisputed, it seems, at times, that the emphasis on the transnational sociocultural system assumes an always increasingly open and counterhegemonic mind, as if the new place would automatically reveal crucial differences, and this in turn would translate into a counterhegemonic rearrangement of public discourses of the self.

New viewpoints can enhance disidentifications, but it would be prudent to pause before blindly believing in the mystical powers of borderlands. Muñoz himself makes this caveat: "There are limits to the strategies, tactics and performativities."[88] That is, "counterpublics are not magically and automatically realized through disidentifications, but they are suggested and articulated."[89] Elaborative empathy as a skill ought to be rehearsed with emotional memories circulating in counterhegemonic representational economies. Different renderings of the self show areas of power rendered invisible to certain subjects.

In *Disidentifications*, Muñoz maps acts that publicize and theatricalize an ethics of the self. I propose learning from disidentifications presented as enactments of power. Learning about areas that were made invisible can show a path to possible positive relations of power that are more inclusive, encourage a greater understanding of diverse ways of emotional suffering and empowerment, provide a better assessment of existing possible problems, and so on. The marketplace of multiculturalism that Muñoz mentioned in 1999 has acquired a particular sophistication in the 2020s that might now be called the "marketing" of diversity.[90] We can still learn a great deal from the way in which *Dominicanish* disidentifies.

The performance focuses on in-group and out-group divisions in the establishment of identity categories by addressing common attachment patterns. Disidentification and attachment play a large role in the emotional involvement elicited by this performance. Attachment patterns inform learned emotions and form emotional memories. Following attachment theory, Hatfield and Rapson demonstrated that "people's love schemas" are in part "shaped by children's early experiences and thus are relatively permanent."[91] Obviously, they are not immutable and may be modified by later experiences. Emotional memories might be learned memories by way of mimetic behavior without representational content; they are not necessarily conscious. These emotions can even precede our capabilities to form episodic memories in early childhood.[92] In *Dominicanish* the hardships are there, mixed in between the words, but meaning is there to be grasped by those who can. Except for very few moments, among them, ten seconds in which Báez sings one of the Isley Brothers' songs, it is clear the artist is there to show her artistic work, not to entertain or move us. The exploration of memory at times avoids the episodic by jumping into lexical transferences, but the emotional memories remain.

The disidentification *Dominicanish* produces turns on their heads the emotional patterns of racism and discrimination in the societies Báez inhabits: American in the DR, Hispanic in America, Black in America, Black in the DR, Black American in the DR, Black Dominican in the Dominican community in New York. All these milieus demand emotional patterns not always in tune with one another. Báez quickly learned that love would have to begin within herself: "Nadie me quiere, coño me quiero yo. ¿Latina me? Latino Theater? They don't look like me. No. African American they are not named Josefina . . . Los blancos ni te digo, el europeo ni te digo . . . entonces . . . yo no voy a pelear con eso. I am not here to fight ignorance. I am not here to teach anybody. I am here to do my best. So, then I have to continue, I give birth to myself."[93] The disidentification also permits audience members to test their own categorizations and learned emotions in reference to any of the experiences perceived in the performance. It is neither a simulation nor a dissimulation; it is simply one instance of productive identity-in-difference.

We have seen how self-definition and self-valuation challenge externally imposed stereotypes. *Dominicanish* nonconfrontationally performs self-valuation in a way that debunks dualistic thinking. Like Muñoz's disidentification and Casamayor-Cisneros's occurrence, self-definition and self-valuation do not discard definitions; they just work with them. The actor/author restructures her power by means of a disidentification with externally imposed expectations. Rather than calling these expectations out, Báez pleasantly ignores them. She acknowledges the externally imposed images she rejects, but that does not constitute the theme of her creative work.

Memories are an integral part in our efforts at elaborative empathy. They serve to evaluate the externally defined images we bring as we approach other spaces of the self. Emotional memories highlight this aspect of "working-with" that we bring with us in our evaluations. Puzzlement can help break the associations attached to particular identity groups that occlude our efforts to understand difference. We mentioned previously that self-definition also rejects internalized images. Here we can see how Báez creates a whole outer and inner space, to then occupy it as author, as performer, and as researcher of the space for herself. I argue that her research offers the "other" the nourishment that confusion can bring in fertile soil, with the ground for empathy cultivated by each other. For its growth to be sustainable, empathy has to be cultivated within. The experience of confusion, here, respects both the self and the other while aerating questions, as new, unforeseen problems arise.

3

Empathy and White Affect

The new Team Sunshine play called ¡*Bienvenidos Blancos!*—in English, *Welcome, White People!*— starts off
as loopy fun with an American couple visiting Cuba;
switches to mystical storytelling that involves the
Cuban revolution and a woman who flees to Miami;
then ends with a deeply felt and poignant declaration about identity from the show's Cuban-American
director Alex Torra. —WHYY.org

THIS CHAPTER FOCUSES ON the theater play ¡*Bienvenidos Blancos!
or Welcome White People!* to examine how feelings entail subject positions. Its methodological lens is centered around the "commons
of the brown," which José Esteban Muñoz posed as an alternative
to white affect.[1] For Muñoz, the "commons" refers to a theoretical
and practical attempt to think spaces of interaction outside the privatization of social life and global capitalism, and "brown" is the
negative space of whiteness. The emotional experiences of Cubans
in exile that this play explores are loaded with additional layers of
conflictive memories. In its four parts one can observe how each

actor diagrams a subject position of their own in a piece that has been collectively crafted. If one considers this play as an enactment of power, it is evident that it allows the director to disidentify with past prejudices and collaborate with subjects raised under divergent ideological positions. In these enactments of power the scenario is one of intercultural understanding, or, as Meghan M. Hammond calls it, a concern for "the conceptual problem of other minds."[2]

Alex Torra, in his play *¡Bienvenidos Blancos!*, worked with Cuban actors from the island and Cuban American actors to create a collaborative piece about Cuba. By exploring this participatory approach to creation and its aim at fostering intercultural dialogs we can think through the problem of participatory empathy, a type of empathy in which the self works together with the other, in this case to create an artistic product. I call it participatory empathy to highlight the physicality and intimate quotidian interaction and knowledge acquisition around agency within the social that participation invokes. It is here that the emotional aspect of empathy clearly unfolds, for "emotions do not just shape how we interpret the world, but also shape which aspects of the world need our attention and which can be safely ignored: emotions are not just about what is, but also about what matters."[3] By analyzing the creative process behind *¡Bienvenidos Blancos! or Welcome White People!*, we see that emotional participation is a crucial element for the artists participating in a common project. Emotional participation in another's experience is here seen as a bridge to civility to "drive home the point that feeling is an important component of empathy."[4] Co-participation expands the possibilities for developing intercultural empathy.

By focusing on how co-participation expands intercultural empathy's conditions of possibility, one cannot but remember Eve Sedgwick's invocation of the tactile plus the emotional in *Touching Feeling: Affect, Pedagogy, Performativity*. Here Sedgwick recommends to "shift the emphasis away from a fixation on epistemology (which suggests that performativity/performance can show us whether or not there are essential truths and how we could, or why we can't, know them) by asking questions about phenomenology and affect (what motivates performativity and performance, for example, and what individual and collective affects are mobilized in their execution?)."[5] The implications of what is "touching" plus the emotional negotiations it demands while collectively creating are palpable. The effort of imagination becomes the effort of collaboration, negotiation, and conviviality—in short, a real, tangible, at times messy, genuine intercultural understanding.

The Play

> Theater artist Alex Torra and Team Sunshine Performance Corp. present this Spanish-language, ensemble-devised performance work that examines privilege, exploitation, and the complexities of Cuban American history and cultural identity. Drawing on Torra's personal experience as a Cuban American, the work "endeavors to make apparent the particularities of a certain corner of the current American landscape—that of the Latino American with one foot in their ethnic heritage and one in a dominantly white culture." Devised by a collective of Cuban, Cuban American, and Caucasian American performers, the project explores Cuba's long history of appeasing/revolting against dominantly white nations and economic forces, including the U.S. The piece showcases how this history has shaped the ways contemporary individuals of Cuban descent understand themselves and their culture.[6]

As soon as the first actor speaks, we learn this is a show that "will make us all learn what is Cuba here [indicating the head/mind] and here [indicating the heart]" (Hoy vamos a conocer qué es Cuba aquí y aquí). The title *Welcome White People!* already states the division between white people and Cuban people. This is further highlighted by the fact that the Cuban actors playing two of the main characters are Black, and the white actors are American. The play explores sardonically and critically the emotional experiences that inform exile and what is said about it today. It is apparent that the actors, working as a collective, have contributed different parts, and these parts do not necessarily share a common view about Cuba.

For Torra, it is an opportunity to deal with different experiences of Cubanness. For the Cuban actors, it is an opportunity to reflect on Cubanness outside the island. The act of working together, rehearsing together, and creating together goes beyond merely uttering the other side of the Cuban experience.

Welcome White People! was part of the April 2018 Fringe Festival in Philadelphia. The opening act of the performance was live music by the percussion collective Timbalona, a group that played at the 2020 performance at Swarthmore College as well. For a good twenty minutes, as people were arriving, the group played Cuban rumba. The stage was set with a desk, a poster of Che Guevara, and photos. Then, as we are taking it all in, a chant to the Yoruba deity Ochun begins, followed by a chant to Eleggua (a Yoruba deity that opens and closes roads) and Obbatala (a Yoruba deity of wisdom and patience). On the one hand, this is in tune with expectations of an ethnic Cuba presented by a Black subject who sings, dances, and entertains the audience. On the other, Yoruba Orishas are an integral part of the culture, so why shouldn't they be there? Indeed, they have to be there. As the acts unfold around the themes of travel, exile, and death, we see that these Orishas make sense. A slide projector is used to mark the beginning of each act and to project supertitles and commentaries. The supertitles add tongue-in-cheek comments that are refreshing and at times very funny: "No time for another drink, if you leave now you miss the beginning, somebody will have to explain it to you . . . Shut up and stop bothering . . ." As they are not identical in Spanish and English, they also allow the performers to get a read on the audience, to see if the majority are bilingual or Latinx, for example.

The first act, "Cuba Wow," sets the dualities that structure the rest of the play. This first act shows the stark contrast between daily life in Cuba and Cuba's exported image. Here, two white tourists arrive at a gloomy tourism office. Soon the ambience shifts to a carnival atmosphere. The employees (Lori Felipe Barkin and Idalmis García) ask the tourists (Benjamin Camp and Jenna Horton) what they want, and the response is typical: the beach, history, dancing, and old cars. Meanwhile, the phrase "We want to go to Cuba before it changes" is projected. This common phrase is often dreaded because Cubans living on the island do want change, and it reads as a cruel petition for frozen time. Numerous language games follow in which locals have fun with the tourists and their inability to understand Spanish. In one instance, the employees at the tourist office make the tourists affirm that in Cuba there is no racism, training them to answer "racism" when the former say, "there is no . . ." Later, when one says, "We want your . . ." the tourist, unaware that the game changed, completes the sentence with "racism" once again, instead of "contribution." In reality, these language games show an exchange of desires in the symbolic realm of Cuba.

One of the tourists notes that "they are poor, but happy," and that he feels free there. This emotional disposition of the tourist enterprise in Third World countries is mocked, as is the demand to be grateful to Fidel. At some point, an actor commands, "Everybody should be grateful because I made Cuba the best place in the world." What follows is an act of impersonation edging on psychological torture, in which the Black Cuban woman makes the white tourist in a Fidel Castro costume apologize for fifty years of dictatorship. This is the moment in which Black and white conflate two realities, one in which white is bad and another one in which white is foreign. As Torra explained on one occasion to an actor, "*You absorb all the ugly, you talked about all the whiteness*, it has to be ugly, the chapter has to be ugly and has to be on point for this moment, we are talking about race, we are talking about money, about class."[7] It is the tensest act in the performance and ends with the other Cuban actor, Jorge Caballero, screaming that the people that want change in Cuba have to demand that change from within Cuba. He yells out, "¡Dictadura Pinochet!" a common saying in Cuba that contests the idea that Cuba is a dictatorship.

This initial portion of the play debunks the myth of the happy tropical island and questions the epic of liberation from afar. Multiple subject positions engage in this questioning: people on the island who have something to lose if they talk too much and who are tired of receiving instructions from Cubans abroad; people who favor noninterventionism; people who defy salvific non-committed postures; and people who want change to come from within Cuba or who want to point out that it is easier said than done to debunk the idea, common in the conservative US, that Cubans are not free because they don't deserve freedom, as if freedom is something that one has to "deserve."

The second act ("Let's Make a Deal") tells the history of a house and the avoidance of death by means of a pact with Eleggua/Eshú. The act is subdivided into parts that are stories featuring Eleggua and Obbatalá as characters, and ends with the history of a house, a history that continues to unfold throughout the rest of the play.

The third act is about departures and arrivals. Here everybody leaves the island. Repeated farewell scenes are played in a loop over and over to the point that the humans in this cycle of departures act like automatons. In a testimonial scene, the New York–based Cuban actress Idalmis García criticizes the Revolution but also portrays life in the United States as very abusive. It is as if that image of the Campbells that Cabrera Infante crafted so well and that appeared in the more recent film *Jirafas* (2015) is replayed over and over when talking about "the Americans." The act ends by talking about suicide, apathy, and struggle. García attributes her grandmother's suicide to an event after which she "dejó de creer en la propaganda," (stopped believing the propaganda) and asserts: "Apathy and a yearning for no more struggle, these feelings are held by many Cubans here and there." At one of the performances, an old Cuban woman walked out on this part of the monologue while screaming "Viva la Revolución, coño!" This was the only incident in response to the performance. As Torra told me, at Fringe they were dealing with a mostly progressive Philadelphia audience; people mostly kept their opinions to themselves.

The fourth act compares the revolution with an engagement. Here the intertextual source for whiteness could have been the hysterical white woman in the classic film *Memories of Underdevelopment* (1968). In the play, as in the film, the white woman makes a scene because her husband decides to stay as she leaves with the first wave of Cuban exiles in the sixties, a group that was overwhelmingly white. In the play, the Black actor Jorge Caballero, who earlier had condemned critics of Cuba coming from outside, did not once step out of a sentimentalist key in this long scene. Looking at his overall performance in this play and being familiar with the dynamics of collective creation, I wonder if this sentimentalism was a solution suggested by the director because the actor did not want to perform anything that would cause him trouble (because he is still based in La Habana), or because the actor rejected any performance of pathos, or "autocannibalism," as Anzaldúa explains: "Perhaps like me you are tired of suffering and talking about suffering. . . . Like me you may be tired of making a tragedy of our lives. . . . *Let's abandon this autocannibalism: rage sadness, fear.*"[8] Miguel Algarín called this self-representational situation the digestion of the self.[9] Part of the negotiations underway in this last act pertain to the fact that while one part of the cast is fiercely anti-Fidel, others don't feel it fits their purpose to share the ugly side of Cuba and prefer to share the goodness.

At the end of the play, during the applause, Torra appears on stage to talk to the public. He explains that in this play, he wanted to discover what it means to be Cuban and if there was a version of Cubanness appropriate for him. He also pointed out that his mother, a Cuban exile from the sixties, was in the audience.

The duality of white versus Cuban does not really address white Cubans or Cuban Americans. Rather, whiteness in the duality refers to naive tourists with dollars and no mastery of the Spanish language or understanding of Cubans. Language is a crucial separator in this color line, as is unfamiliarity with Cuban society. Given that the duality is posed in terms of color, racism and the difficulty Afro-Cubans have in leaving the island or receiving remittances could have merited a scene. Asked about this, Torra noted that selecting Cuban actors who were Black was not conscious; it just so happened that the two people cast for the performance seemed like the most qualified, as they both had a lot of experience working with improvisation and creating work device processes. "Race was a consideration, but it was not a top consideration. It was like we should be aware of it, but really we are looking for people who would fit in

devising processes."[10] The performance questions American privilege, according to Torra, but the figure of the Cuban American
in Cuba remains absent.[11] Perhaps Torra's confusion over feeling
like a white tourist and also feeling Cuban explains this conflation.

Alex Torra is one of the three Team Captains in the artist group
Team Sunshine. Team Sunshine Performance Corporation is a Philadelphia based company dedicated to serving as a hub for the imaginative consideration of contemporary American culture and what
it means to be a participant in it. (Company's Mission statement)
Theatre and dance artists Benjamin Camp, Makoto Hirano, and Alex
Torra founded the company in 2010, which has been incorporated
since 2015. The way that this company works is that every project has
a lead artist (Ben, Makoto or Alex). That lead artist has a starting idea,
"usually something that feels unresolved in their system, and then the
collective creative process would help to unstick it, and to move, we
use the process as a way of break it open and then move it into something that can be shared publicly, and would be theatrically viable."[12]

The Problem of Other Minds

In-group/out-group relations have a bearing on personal predisposition to empathy. Patrick Hogan talks about inhibited empathy,
and Sarah Cavanaugh mentions the studies of Beckes, Coan and
Hasselno, but in *Empathy in the Global World*, Calloway-Thomas
goes beyond the cognitive, back into the realm of philosophy.[13] Her
take brings to the fore Hume's concentric circles of empathy. The
concept of concentric circles of loyalty and empathy is that human
beings love and are loyal to their families first, and then their loyalty
diminishes as they move from the center to the periphery.[14] These
circles of empathy account for a phenomenon not unlike the Stoic
oikeiosis, "the notion that we prefer those closest to ourselves than
those farthest away."[15] Here in-group relations constitute the center
and out-group relationships are spatially imagined as on the outskirts. Calloway-Thomas advocates for a leap, so to speak, out of
these constraints in the era of globalization, which has considerably

affected the limits determining what is close or distant from our selves. Calloway-Thomas sets up her work to inquire about "the extent to which individuals are indeed practicing empathy at this critical juncture in history, the juncture of globalization."[16] The practice of intercultural empathy today, the author claims, cannot ignore the magnitude of information available about the "other," but "part of empathy's work then is to knit together human and cultural elements of both the near and the distant so that we will care about other people even if they are an ocean away."[17] Calloway-Thomas mentions the work of Giambattista Vico, who proposed an imaginative process to allow one to "leave one's own world and enter into the world of the other" which implied the need for "a sufficient effort of imagination."[18] Leaving one's world to enter a world of equal collaboration with the other can expand empathic thought in a world where the imagination is bombarded with very specific messages based on identity.

A quest for an appropriate version of Cubanness mobilized Torra to embark on the creative process that resulted in ¡Bienvenidos Blancos! or Welcome White People! Torra asserts that he never really felt Latino enough because he is white and had a different immigration experience than many other Latinxs, but, at the same time, he never truly fit into Miami's Little Havana, where he is from: "I didn't fit in the Cuban American world in Miami; I always felt a little bit weird because I was an artist. I didn't come out as queer when I was a kid, but I am, and I felt it. I was a sensitive boy in a world in which masculinity is hard, so I didn't quite fit."[19]

But once he escaped this Miami world, he entered into the "very white universe of theater."[20] He says he adapted to it, changing his accent from "Miami" to "American" in order to be a stage actor. "That was fine. All I wanted was to be a theater person, and that is how you succeeded, which is versing yourself in white theater, acting in white plays, directing them." But then, the spate of "very public murders of Black people by the police" that occurred in 2014 and 2015 opened a dialogue at the national level, and at that moment Torra began to feel the need to understand:

Where does my kind of Latino fit in this picture, and where [do] Latinx cultures fit in this. Right around there, I started to feel that in order to figure out how I fit in this cultural moment, I needed to figure out my relation to being Cuban and to being a white Cuban American. This was at the beginning of the Black Lives Matter movement, and I asked myself, how do I fit in this? How do I authentically live inside this world? I was like: I have to figure out my Cuban stuff.[21]

When he got the opportunity to travel to Cuba, a new world opened up. He went there for the first time in October 2015 to prepare a funding application for the play and to "process Cuban culture."[22] He wanted to break free of the inherited narrative about Cuba. Since most of his understanding of Cuban culture and history had been filtered through his parents, he wanted to create his own opinions and perspective. For that, he wanted to include people who represented his own identity, so he chose to work with Cuban American artists, with Cuban artists, and with white American artists. Once he received a Pew Foundation grant, he began to travel regularly to the island, first to cast Cuban actors, then for rehearsals, and, later, to rework parts of the play, a new version of which was performed at Swarthmore College in January 2020. Torra commented that as a Cuban American, "you are not supposed to go to Cuba; I was nervous about it and scared."[23] Asked if he felt treated as white in Cuba, he said yes, but also noted a lack of definition: "When I am in Cuba, I am not really a tourist, and I am not really Cuban, I am like somewhere in between, but I am treated as both all the time, and I get really confused."[24] Part of this experience is reflected in the play's first act, or chapter, as the acts are called in the play itself. One could argue that this play is a way of seeking a perspective for understanding not only why people think and behave as they do, but also why the self does so.[25]

In *Against Race: Imagining Political Culture*, Paul Gilroy notes that the term "identity" has been part of a scholarly vocabulary "designed to promote critical reflection upon who we are and what we want."[26] For Torra, understanding the differences in how we think of identity was part of the collaborative process:

> The kinds of images and words, and things that are coming to me about my Cuban American world are completely different from what Cubans in the island experience, and so it is not just intellectual, it is *emotional, it's like spiritual, there is all these textures and feelings that are hard to summarize into language.* They don't define or practice the defining of identity exactly the same way. It is a different relationship to that identity, but to even understand that there is a different relationship to that identity takes time, and then to take the time to figure out what is the difference in the relationship to that identity, that is a huge, long process.[27]

According to Gilroy, the idea of identity helps to comprehend the formation of that perilous pronoun "we" and to "reckon with the pattern of inclusion and exclusion that it cannot help creating."[28] Jennine Capó Crucet, a Cuban American writer, did as much when she wrote *My Time among the Whites*. There are two passages that shed light on Torra's stated intentions of discovering what it means to be Cuban:

> Thanks to the fantasy of Cuba our families built in our minds, a Cuba we could never know even if we grew up to someday visit it, we were well practiced in longing for places where, as the song promises, anything your heart desires will come to you.[29]

> Because in Miami the white experience is also typically a Cuban one: to be Cuban in Miami was to be kind of white, with all the privileges and sense of cultural neutrality whiteness affords.[30]

The theme of the fantasy clearly resonates with Torra, who sees it as a structural element of Cuban life along a winding timeline: the fantasy of the Revolution started in 1959, the Miamian Cuban fantasy that "Cuba will be ours again," and now the white fantasy. "I went to Cuba, and there was this thing I hate, the back of the coco

FIGURE 3.1 Idalmis García and Jorge Caballero in ¡*Bienvenidos Blancos!* Photo by Kate Raines/ Plate 3 Photography.

taxi says 'rentar una fantasía,' and I was like that is what we are doing here, *we are renting a fucking fantasy* to a bunch of Americans. This is when Cuba was starting to open up to the US."[31] The title of the play, then, comes as no surprise, dealing with different takes on white affect or this preoccupation with caring about people *an ocean away*. For many Cuban Americans, physical distance between the diaspora and the island entails cultural and ideological differences that disorient closed notions of identity once the *problem of other minds* arises on the horizon.

The problem of other minds that Hammond sees as a new concern in many nineteenth-century literatures (Romanticism, realism, naturalism, modernism) is, for Calloway-Thomas, a civic issue in the twenty-first century. Both Calloway-Thomas and Hammond establish different ways of relating to other minds and needs. For Hammond, the shift from sympathetic to empathic models marks the psychology of modernism. Calloway-Thomas, on the other hand, differentiates between hard and soft empathy to attend to the different modes of empathic engagement present in global politics.

Soft empathy refers to mostly obligatory work that results in a short-term relief of suffering and hard empathy, in turn, brings in an attentiveness to local concerns, an understanding of the social setting, trustworthiness, and visions of independence.[32] She is concerned with empathy as that which sustains civil society, constituting and promoting human dignity. The problem of other minds here is a problem related to empathetic practices across a range of cultures and geopolitical international policies. For Calloway-Thomas, empathy is "the ability 'imaginatively' to enter into and participate in the world of the cultural other cognitively, affectively and behaviorally."[33] While I do not propose that the play *¡Bienvenidos Blancos! or Welcome White People!* acts as a template, it is pertinent to study its creative process as having the potential to be considered as a new intersubjective consciousness that underwent construction. Calloway-Thomas borrows the concept of intersubjectiveness from Yuval Noah Harari's *Sapiens*, explaining that Harari differentiates between the subjective, which is individual and rests heavily on beliefs, and the intersubjective, which exists within a communication network.[34] Along the two kinships that Cuban-Americans must often navigate, we can see how disidentification with inherited prejudices and obstructed empathetic response (to determined realities around the Cuban experience and identity) play at both the subjective and intersubjective levels.

Calloway-Thomas contends that communication programs at both the high school and university levels should have lessons and units that model how citizens are supposed to behave in the presence of others.[35] Torra experimented with these issues from rehearsal to rehearsal, when the cast, comprising subjects with dissimilar ideological views of Cuba, met frequently to participate in the creative process, therefore sustaining regular intercultural encounters that could potentially deossify discourse in America about Cubanness, and in Cuba about Americanness. To be clear, the empathetic literacy that underwent construction has more to do with the act of collective creation and rehearsal than with representation, although every performance opens varied intersubjective

FIGURE 3.2 *¡Bienvenidos Blancos!* rehearsal in 2017. Photo by Kate Raines/Plate 3 Photography.

channels. When in *My Time among the Whites*, Capó Crucet positions herself in relationship to "the problem of empathy" she asserts: "I tell readers that I see it as my job to tell stories that encourage people to *act* on their empathy—not just to *feel* something."[36] In *¡Bienvenidos Blancos! or Welcome White People!*, acting on empathy is both figurative and literal. The actress Jenna Horton considers the creative rehearsal experience to be "so fundamental, creating friendships with those folks in the room simultaneously. It was so rewarding in some ways, being so close. The physicality of being close to those stories is so much different than the white culture of reading it in the textbook, like a total abstraction, which is very much how I grew up and learned up to now about US history as a white person. That was so much clearer, even if difficult; so much closer, so much more active. It was rewarding."[37] Cheryl Zaldívar, the Cuban assistant director, explained during the Q&A at Swarthmore that followed the performance in 2020, "We tried to expand our minds to connect with each other and that was the actual engine of the whole show. It is the first time that I know of that this has been done." Although we cannot obviate the fact that collaboration is in this case a labor relationship where actors and staff are paid for their time in Cuba and in America by one of the parts, Alex, collaboration in this play enacts collective empowerment and intercultural understanding.

Enactments of Power and Intercultural Understanding

In the 2018 Fringe performances, the last three acts of the play were about the emotional experiences of exile. When the second act was revamped in 2020, the history of the house became a *pataki* (Yoruba sacred story), and the whole second part (acts 2–4) put more emphasis on resilience and resistance than on emotional memories of exile. The differences shed light on Torra's path toward cultural understanding and the negotiations occurring in a space of collaboration encompassing the "commons of the brown," a space that seeks also to accommodate the negative space of white affect. Caballero, still based in La Habana, had another understanding of his function and intentions in the play, and that had to be worked out. The revamping of act 2 was a way of opening space for Caballero's participation on his own terms. At the Q&A after the Swarthmore performance, he acknowledged this and explained the nature of the task. According to him, the new act 2 was in response to "una búsqueda que planteó Alex de buscar una conexión mía con el objetivo de la obra que fuera más allá del estereotipo" (a personal search that Alex proposed, a search that could connect with the play's goal going beyond stereotypes). Caballero wanted to present in this—his chapter, so to speak—a part of Cuban society. He treasured the opportunity to show his identity, his culture, and his nation, in a form that was ready to share.

The new act presented the audience with a *pataki* depicting a Yoruba version of the history of humanity. The Yoruba religion is how Caballero connects to his racial, cultural, and national identity. It strengthens for him the relationship to what Torra would call "Cubanness." Yoruba and Santeria intercultural encounters and initiations are part of the touristic circuit, providing substantial revenue, so while this is part of the stereotype of Black Cuba in the intercultural and international arena, the stereotype of talking about Cuba in America is, for this Havana-based artist, the daily description of

all types of miseries.[38] The part of Cuban society that is not a stereotype for him is the spiritual relation to a position of power. Dressing all in white while dancing puts him in direct connection with
this power, and many Yoruba followers would treat him accordingly
if he were to go outside dressed this way. Rather than describing
a present he knows all too well, he describes a past that provides
a metanarrative of conflict. He reaffirms a space of internal freedom—a safe space for the self—instead of dealing with what is
outside of the self.

Kevin Delgado provides some relevant historical background
on the position of Santeria within cultural practice and the State's
cultural policy:

> Ironically while the "superstitious" elements of the religion were
> derided during the first decades of the Revolution, the government
> itself provided a means of employment for a few expert practi-
> tioners. Through Santeria was regulated and its practitioners mar-
> ginalized, the religion never came close to disappearing during the
> first decades of the Revolution and in some ways became more vis-
> ible than ever. Since 1985, the Cuban government began operating
> a program for foreigners called Folk Cuba, featuring workshops in
> AfroCuban drumming and dance. As government employees, these
> artists drew a salary in exchange for the study, creation, rehearsal
> and performance of folkloric arts. After Cuba's opening in the 1990s,
> FolkCuba became a template for the expansion of cultural and even
> religious tourism as an economic enterprise. In the Special Period,
> the Afro-Cuban tradition that previously had been folklorized and
> professionalized were increasingly capitalized.[39]

When I interviewed Jorge Caballero, there were many things I
wanted to ask him that I rapidly abandoned, knowing with certainty
that *if* these questions were answered this would compromise his
livelihood in Cuba. Many questions went unanswered as well, and
I did not insist. This is the reality of this intercultural exchange.
My decision could be read as complicity with censorship, but people's lives are more important than a book chapter. Cuba's very

constitution puts limits on artistic freedom: article 38 specifies
that artistic freedom exists provided that its content does not go
against the revolution. The decree 349 further curtailed independent artists' work. Since 2020, the government employed law 370
and law 310 to fine a broad array of people for Facebook comments
criticizing, for example, the way that the government was dealing
with the Covid-19 pandemic.[40] A lot of people are in jail and many
more lost their jobs as a result of "opinions." In July of 2021, thousands took to the streets protesting the government's handling of
coronavirus and the economy. The repressive response resulted in
1000 people incarcerated; 400 of them had been already sentenced
and the rest await trial.[41] What quickly followed was a new decree
establishing regulations on the use of social media and internet.
This decree makes impacting the country's prestige a cyber security
incident that is considered a crime. Under the new rules "no one
can denigrate an official of the country or the revolutionary process."[42] The control always existed, but it is now set in stone through
the penal code.[43] So, when Torra asks Caballero to talk about the
ugly with no results, or mentions that, in discussion happening
during rehearsals, Caballero "doesn't even have an opinion," it is
really not surprising.

Tania Bruguera and Coco Fusco had both called attention to
behavior in performance and in the performance of art criticism.
As the recognized performance artist Tania Bruguera notes, "Art
and politics have many things in common. They both imagine the
future; they both use emotions and manage the power of symbols.
Art like politics affect people."[44] An art event is here "a rehearsal of
reality, as a rehearsal of the future."[45] Echoing this approach, Coco
Fusco stresses the importance of an informed reading of behaviors
in *Dangerous Moves: Performance and Politics in Cuba.*

> Although Cuban art critics now refer to social practice as the
> study of conduct, they do not address Cuba's own political cul-
> ture of visual propaganda, obligatory collective activity, manda-
> tory demonstrations of patriotism, practices of policing and sur-
> veillance—all of which contribute to shaping social conduct. It is

as if the political culture that informs daily life, that has resulted in numerous closings of art exhibitions and that has produced jail sentences for thousands of non-conformists were of no significance at all for endeavours that are essentially expressive.[46]

So, while it is safe for Alex Torra to explore the version of *cubanía* or cubanness that fits his identity, the cultural exchange could not have elicited in Caballero the amplitude of movement to diagram a personal national identity. Yet, both Alex Torra and Jorge Caballero, as different as they are, were dealing in performance with massive public social pressures and the agendas of institutional funding. Torra is free to rethink his connection to the present and the political culture that informs daily life; it is not a dangerous move, but a fructiferous one. That is why it is not the result but the process that can help all involved actors realize how emotions entail subjective positions.

The collaborative work behind the new act fosters skills to manage intercultural encounters caringly and competently, "which in turn allows intercultural empathy."[47] Caballero greatly valued the support of the white American actors, for they helped him share in a manner that generated greater understanding of his culture, presenting the Afro-Cuban myth of the beginning of humanity. He said that by working to be understood, he searched within himself for what he wanted to communicate. They acted as a prototypical audience, anticipating the audience that was now in front of him as he spoke at Swarthmore College.

Empathy and White Affect: Self and Other in Exile

The differences between the 2018 and 2020 versions of the play mark a trajectory in which memories of exile are given less importance. The contribution of Idalmis García (the other Cuban actor) was likewise weakened, in part because she could not perform in the 2020 version but also because the form of delivery was substantially changed. Act 2 ("Let's Make a Deal") combined the history of a deal with Eleggua with a *pataki* and then with the history of a house. In

2020, "Let's Make a Deal" became "Afrocubanía," a twelve-minute *pataki* about the origins of humanity. Act 3 (Departures/Arrivals) continued in the house presented in the third section of act 2. In 2020, García could not perform in act 3, which presented the memories of García herself, who had recently arrived in the US. The Cuban actress Cheryl Zaldívar, who was previously the assistant director, took on her role, but the delivery felt like a flat reading of the previous script. Torra mentioned when I interviewed him that he was trying a technique developed by the Pig Iron Company called "ordinary." It is not quite realism, but a style of lower realism: everyday, quotidian, and nonperformative. It is in a performance, but the performer's intention is not to perform. The section, for whatever reason, comes off as non-performative, but the absence of expression of an emotional connection to the material somehow takes away the ordinary nature of this style as well. It somehow loses impetus with this new technique, an impetus that counterbalanced nicely one of the prevalent topics in this part: apathy. This low realism (if that was the intention behind the delivery) ends up disposing of all realism. The delivery, can nonetheless, be explained outside of this technical rationale. Cheryl Zaldívar's relation to the play in this part feels very different, perhaps because García was putting her own reality in this, and that could be perceived. Zaldívar resides in Cuba, and it seemed she could not, or did not want to, inhabit García's feelings about living outside Cuba. In the new version, arrivals and departures were conflated with the history of a house and the reality of living outside Cuba.[48] It is curious to realize that in the tandem of two white Cuban Americans and two black Cubans that existed initially, the female black Cuban had her voice flattened, and the female Cuban American, had her part obliterated and/or parodied, as we will see.

In order to highlight how feelings entail subject positions, I want to analyze the structures of feeling "attached"—as Sara Ahmed would say—to subjects in act 4 ("Fantasy"), which plays allegorically with a broken engagement. The couple consists of a white woman (Lori Felipe, who according to Torra, was engaging with her grandmother's past in the creative process) and a black man

(Jorge Caballero). The white woman cries because the man will not leave the country to follow her, not wanting to abandon the newly established revolutionary government. Hence the allegory in which one engagement, the couple's, points to another: the revolutionary engagement. The scene, as we mentioned, is reminiscent of a similar one present in *Memories of Underdevelopment* (1968), a movie by Cuban Film director Tomás Gutierrez Alea. In the play, one character is tragically melodramatic and the other is melodramatic in a comic way. It seems as if the comedic mocks the tragic film version in which both the man and woman were white and rich. For the two characters in the play, the same event is encoded differently, or the encoded information begs a different interpretation as a result of markedly different deliveries. Intensity in the white subject is brought to the point of the tragic. The Black subject in the same scene engages by singing a *bolero* to portray a romantically exaggerated sentimentalism. At times, it seems no empathy can result from this form of accounting for events. Torra states that the scene wasn't intended to be parodic, but rather a stylized memory of this woman's past.

Still, the unwillingness of this woman's partner to acknowledge her—even to the point of dismissing her altogether—favors another reading in which acknowledging this parodic aspect gains relevance. For example, Jorge Caballero goes down on one knee and then changes the knee he is resting on to the other one in a funny, rushed way and later coquettishly applies more hair gel in front of an imaginary mirror while the other character cries. To understand the inhibition of empathy through identity categories, Patrick Hogan analyzes the role of encoding and its effect on emotional skills, noting that Blacks and whites placed in the same situations are read differently.[49] Subjects and subject matters endure different readings according to their identity categories. While overemotionalization is dropped at the feet of the white female bourgeois subject, the Black subject is left to play a role that is either comical or cynical, and in that last aspect resembles the white male subject in *Memories of Underdevelopment.* Yet, in the context of Cuban exile, one might say that the white hysterical subject crying about only having two options might seem frivolous to a Black person having only one—which is to say, none.

Here it is evident that while in-group/out-group divisions are pervasive in real life, they are also pervasive in fictional works, as Hogan explains: "Racial, religious, ethnic, national and other ideologies are widespread in literature. Thus, literary works may not only foster an openness to empathy; they may also foster an inhibition of empathy through identity categorization."[50] The play explores different perspectives in the history of Cubanness through a determined negation of white affect. Torra, as a Cuban American, has long been exposed to the narrative of the heartbreaking circumstances of exile. I don't mean they were not heartbreaking, but rather that he might be here exploring other forms of feeling, feeling brown, feeling outside of white affect, forms that do not pertain to the self. Doing this entails learning about other structures of feeling that inform Cubanness. The result was that some voices were lifted and others quieted. The perspective and emotions of the female Cuban American actor-collaborator lose validation.

Feeling is working here as disidentification, much in the way that Michel Pêcheux described it: "the taking up of a non-subjective position" in "historical devices of experimentation-transformation."[51] In the fourth act, the Black character engages in disidentification, taking advantage of structures of domination. In the play as a whole, disidentification allows Alex Torra to "reconstruct his dislocated identity free of learned prejudices."[52] Both ¡Bienvenidos Blancos! and Dominicanish engage in such a reconstruction, yet they do so in the contexts of different national histories. Torra appeared to be fighting both prejudices and whiteness when, during the Swarthmore Q&A, he expressed that, as his Cuban ancestors gradually leave this world (his aunt died in 2019), "I think sometimes they are taking my connection to Cuba with them. And it is possible that little by little I myself am becoming whiter. So, I made this show. But it is complicated."

Torra wanted to include tourism in the performance as a way of dealing with whiteness, and he also wanted to deal with what his Cuban American upbringing had left behind:

I carry in my system as the son of Cubans who came over in the sixties a real racism, like a real Cuban racism. I was like, I need to deal with it and I need, we need, in this story, in this thing we are doing, we need to get rid of an old narrative that says that Yoruba and Santería are the scary part of Cuban culture. Growing up, I notice we don't look at that directly, we can do some songs about it, and then we can secretly put *vasos de agua* underneath the beds and stuff, but we don't talk about it. And I was "no," actually African culture, Yoruba, is like at the core of Cuban culture, it is in there, so it felt important to do that.[53]

A big part of the negotiation in the transit to the new version of this play pertains to the notion of "selling culture," which Torra initially saw as antithetical to the ideals of the revolution and to Cuban dignity. For him, it is a real tragedy to see a culture saying all the time "we are amazing," and at the same time "trying to sell themselves. One of the things I learned in the process, and I think it is one of the things Jorge understands and has absorbed, is that these are not at odds; they just exist at the same time. It doesn't make you less. It doesn't make you less of a person to have to sell yourself or sell your culture."[54] One could also ask if proposing a play about Cuba and whiteness—precisely around 2015's Obama-era changes to Cuba travel policy and Obama's mediatic visit to the country in 2016—does not also enter into a type of profitability, one in which funding might be accomplished by touching on the trendy topics that orient foundations' grant award decisions.

It is key to take in the collaborative effort that the piece entails, for it facilitates *and* complicates disidentification. Torra could be said to belong to the "commons of the brown" that Muñoz articulated in "Feeling Brown" and other works.[55] But, at the same time, it is evident that *¡Bienvenidos Blancos!* explores the subject position of feeling white, or at least deals with white affect. It is an alternate enactment of power that explores the idea that feelings entail subject positions. Cubans in exile might feel brown in America but white when visiting Cuba; brown and white are not colors here: they are predispositions to positions of power and privilege.

These predispositions might not be actualized, yet they still guide perceptions of in-group/out-group relations. Consequently, "[t]he Brown commons is not about the production of the individual but instead about a movement, a flow, and an impulse, to move beyond the singular and individualized subjectivities."[56] Brown, for Muñoz, is everything that does not conform to white affect: "It is first and foremost brown as in brown people in an immediate way; but also many other vulnerable positions, such as people who are rendered brown by a personal or familiar participation in a south to north migration pattern. Or, people who are brown by way of accents and linguistic orientations that convey a certain difference, also, brown conferred by the way spatial coordinates are contested; or how one's right to residency is challenged."[57] Similarly to Anzaldúa's *Borderlands*, Muñoz is presenting brown affect as more complex, defying the idea of a subject defined by the lack of something.

White affect characterizes a certain static mental framework that can only envision victims and villains but nothing in between. Defying white affect in performance provides modes of collective disidentification. The fourth act in *Welcome White People!* can be read in different ways, but it is clear that white affect is not there to be pampered. When the hysterical white woman cries and complains when her fiancée or husband decides to stay in Cuba, she is performed in a way that elicits no empathy because of a bourgeois quality being attached to a color. The Black subject, on the other hand, plays an overly melodramatic character, so exaggerated that he can only be taken to be a parody of white affect. Yet, some people in the audience connected with the allegory of the broken heart of people "engaged with" the revolution, which is also part of the emotional memories available. In fact, it might be that encoding the white character's performance as exaggerated is a result of the other character's response. Here, it is interesting how certain emotional memories or experiences predispose people to perceive or overrule parody because of the allegory sustaining it.

I asked Torra about what emotional experience he was able to explore more fully by working collectively on this play. He stated that one element of the Cuban experience he got to delve into was

FIGURE 3.3 Scene from *¡Bienvenidos Blancos!* rehearsal. Photo by Kate Raines/Plate 3 Photography.

apathy; apathy is "a significant quality of the Cuban experience. To me it has never been part of it because my understanding of being Cuban is you fight, keep fighting, then keep fighting . . . but I didn't understand that really actually secretly inside of me—and others—a lot of us have given up. That is a huge part of it."[58] Particularly elucidating was García's collaboration, which brought about this new understanding of apathy previously unknown to Torra. Apathy has "the potential to hack and reconfigure well-worn affective dynamics to still other possibilities," it is a sort of rerouting of destructively intense emotional engagement.[59]

Empathy in Our America

The artistic project behind *¡Bienvenidos Blancos! or Welcome White People!* began, according to Torra, when events highlighting police brutality in 2014 and 2015 sparked the Black Lives Matter movement. These events set in motion Torra's inquiry about whiteness and Cubanness. The project reached closure with its last performance in January 2020. I met with him for an interview in June 2020, just weeks after the wave of public protests over the killing of George Floyd by a police officer in Minneapolis. Given that the mission of Sunshine Company encompasses "serving as a hub for the imaginative consideration of contemporary American culture and what it means to be a participant in it," it's impossible not to set an analysis of the play against that background. Torra's inquiry into identity and whiteness resonated with the current collective quest for thinking about white affect in our experience of America and about the commons of the brown, where different feelings can denote different subject positions.

Just as police violence against Black people caused Torra to think about his relationship to white America and to whiteness, the notion of America employed in the collaborative process needs to be read against the grain of more recent events related to BLM. Jody David Armour, professor of Law at the University of Southern California since 1995, points to this America when he remarks that if an attack on the police is an attack on America (as LAPD police chief Charlie Beck asserted) then,

> by the same token, an unjustified attack by a police officer on a black person is an attack by America on that individual. You know, that was America shooting Walter Scott in the back in South Carolina a few years back and 12-year-old Tamir Rice in Cleveland. And that was America choking Eric Garner to death as he gasped, I can't breathe, in New York. And that was America, I think many people saw, digging its knee into the neck of George Floyd as he gasped his last breath in Minnesota.[60]

This is the same America and the same dialogue about whose lives matter that, as mentioned above, moved Torra to search for his Cubanness to resolve how he fit in this picture, this cultural moment. In May and June 2020, a very palpable contraposition to white affect and whiteness as "a state of mind—dualistic, supremacist, separatist, hierarchical"—occupied the streets of America, obeying a form of participatory empathy against white supremacy never seen before in white America to such a degree.[61] The supremacist,

separatist, hierarchical mind, which Gloria Anzaldúa was working to transform, is part of the legacy of racism that, according to
Torra, was transplanted from Cuba to the Miami where he grew
up.[62] Empathy was, at that moment, operating under the commons of the brown posited by Muñoz, not to think of alternative
spaces to white affect but to highlight the brutality of the spaces
left available to the commons of the brown.

When José Martí, then living in New York in 1891, wrote his
essay "Nuestra América," he was looking to awaken the empathy
of his fellow Latin Americans to the cause of Cuban independence,
by reasserting their common battle against the predatory nature
of expansionist capitalism. The United States was "their" America, for Martí, the sort of America that later became "our America" for many Cubans in exile since the sixties. Martí's experience
of being an outsider within is quintessential to Martí's writings.
"America" is here not only a terrain; it's an approach to identity.[63]
For Martí, appealing to a common threat was a way to incentiv-
ize an empathetic response. His essay was, in part, contesting an
assessment of US foreign policy actions that interpreted them as
isolated, "occasional" breaches of sovereignty.

In the case of George Floyd's murder—at the hands of three
police officers arresting him for a supposedly counterfeit twenty-
dollar bill—the claim that it was an isolated case could no longer
hold. As a result, according to Jody David Armour, there is greater
societal empathy now than when police brutality was first caught
on video in 1992:

> The protests and marches today you see are multiethnic, multicul-
> tural, even multigenerational. And the allyship is something that
> is more pronounced now than it perhaps once was. You know, I
> think a lot of people, when they saw that video of George Floyd,
> who weren't in the black community felt agony. And I think this
> time around, more people feel that sympathy and empathy for
> members of the black community and are standing in solidarity
> with them.
>
>   I think at the time of the Rodney King beating, it was easier to
> view it as an isolated incident or as a few bad apples, right? But

now, over time, we see a persistent and pervasive pattern—right?—
over years and years.[64]

Watching the recorded death of George Floyd suddenly united a
large number of Americans in protests repudiating police brutality. And that resulted in more police brutality exercised on demonstrators—large numbers of protesters and media professionals
now have firsthand experience of it—making it even more difficult
to deny or attribute to chance. If we conflate police with America
and America with justice, one cannot fail to see that justice is unsay-
ing itself by the very police attacks whose only apparent purpose
seems to be to break the dignity and bodies of the persons they target—attacks that, when exercised on white bodies, are classified
as human rights violations. On January 6, 2021, any initial justice
response against an attempted coup d'état seemed absent and the
police brutality that one would have likely seen were these demonstrators not white supremacists and far-right groups excused
itself from the date. What became even more evident that day is
that America does not assign equal rights to all bodies. If we want
to read the situation in terms of empathic responses, we need to
understand not only the victims but also the conditions of possibility for the existence of unequal subject positions.

The idea of a "true America" that is white is certainly part of
white affect.[65] On June 2, I tuned in to WRTI, Temple University's
radio station based in North Philadelphia, to listen to the Bob Perkins Jazz Show, which was dedicated that day to discussing the
protests, Black lives, and Black music as a form of social engagement. Empathy and mandatory cultural exchanges were among
the solutions envisioned by the pianist Orrin Evans and the bass-
ist, composer, and arranger Christian McBride in their conversation with Bob Perkins about Black lives and the power of Black
music. The three were saying that after Rodney King, Trayvon Martin, and Michael Brown, nothing changed, and perhaps what was
needed was a moment in which being white means being outside of
the majority. McBride proposed a mandatory cultural exchange in
which the privileged live with the nonprivileged "to change people's

hearts given that seeing people dying on camera is not enough."[66] A white musician that used to play basketball on an all-Black team talked about how that experience made him feel like a minority, a feeling that he had carried with him since then. Evans, who plays in the band The Bad Plus, where he is "the only one that looks like me," provided another anecdote. A fan of the band once told Evans that, as a "true American," he had been concerned when Evans joined the band and didn't know if it was going to work. However, the fan told him, Evans "is ok." Commenting on this, and never using the word "black," the radio interviewers and the guests kept talking until Evans, referring to the fan, asked what would happen "if you could step in my shoes for one moment."

Claudia Rankine asks if conversations are pathways to the exchange of understandings; in this part of *Just Us*, she was engaging with Samuel Beckett, who once said that "writing *Waiting for Godot* was a way of finding a form that accommodates the mess."[67] Perhaps the answer lies in the coexistence of words and affect that staging discomfort allows. Bretton White's theatrical approach focuses on the affective experience of the audience, an affective experience outside the realm of words and meaning. This might not paint the whole picture that participatory empathy unfolds, but it certainly brings intelligibility to the place of Latinxs in the US racial American landscape in terms of belonging. Rankine notes that many consider "Latinx and Asian people as the 'junior partners' in a white nationalist administration."[68] The case of Latino member involvement with the Proud Boys comes to mind, but there are many other possible examples. Not surprisingly, marginalized subjects might want to advance toward the centers of power taking in their discourses of legitimacy.[69] Participatory empathy proposes the opposite move, and it might open a path for understanding in reverse; it is a vector that goes in the other direction. "Theater and performance [can be] a multi-sited transnational practice in which authors, actors, and audiences make temporary homes for bodies and discourses not always recognized by the majoritarian culture of the nation-state."[70] "Perhaps words are like rooms; they have to make room for people."[71] Words, such as our America (in English), remind us that it is not only a matter of "recognition," but of aggressive and calculated exclusion in a game of diversity without pluralism. Perhaps performance is a way of making room, and rehearsals are a way of finding a form that accommodates the mess.

"It took fucking forever"

Collective collaborative enactments of power, if done right, disempower individual certainties. Calloway-Thomas (2018), like Susan Lanzoni (2018), sees empathy as a toolbox with very definite functions: to sustain civil society and human dignity by imagining a new intersubjective consciousness, to give others the benefit of perceptual doubt, and to create intersubjective imaginaries.[72] Empathy cannot evolve properly without sustained contact with other subjectivities. I have noticed the difficulty of doing this in my own teaching. Aside from issues concerning comfort, "being in the world" involves real safety concerns. Yet, we can find a suitable negotiation between safety and intercultural understanding in the scenario presented by the production of *¡Bienvenidos Blancos! or Welcome White People!*

The production of *¡Bienvenidos Blancos! or Welcome White People!* negotiates this line between safety and intercultural understanding through rehearsals that encompass both sustained effort and a certain level of equality. One aspect of power privilege is the inability or lack of incentive to listen to other experiences. Tim Wise in *White Like Me* highlights the problem: white folks "have never trained to listen to brown and black folks when they talk about their reality and to believe they know about it." In order to get past this, "they have to learn to listen, learn to believe, to trust that they know their reality."[73] This effort of imagination and dedication to listening was, Torra noted, one of the most challenging elements of working together across Cuban cultures:

> The thing that was hard, the difficulty . . . is . . . *it is really hard to know what you don't know.* At a meeting I had questions, you know . . . when you are making work over time, there is a collective vocab-

ulary, not just about performance but about the content itself. So, like talking about Cuban history, *one's relationship to Cuban history* and the images and the moments, and the political dynamics, and the racial dynamics, and the class distinctions, all this stuff is different in the US than it is in Cuba, right? *We are looking at this thing in the middle from different perspectives.* So trying to get to the same perspective or understand each other's perspectives, *it took fucking forever.*[74]

We have seen that the creative process in this theatrical piece began with an encounter with the Cuban American director's self in the United States, followed by an encounter with this self abroad in Cuba, and ending with the emotional experiences of empathy in America. Rereading his Cuban American self allows Torra, and his audiences, to identify prejudices and blind spots, unknown predispositions toward identity. The way the performance brings the self to other worlds, in this case Cuba as an island, but also as a space of identity's experience, allows us to put Torra's work in conversation with white people's recent participation in protests against police brutality. America is here a divided continent where capitalism and whiteness need to be reexamined. Participatory empathy demands collaboration, and sometimes, as the rehearsals and reiterations of this play demonstrated, a concern for the other in creative terms; that is, actually creating results in which once one listens, actions follow. "Feeling white," but not quite white, opened the doors for this playwright to reexamine his identity and proactively and practically engage empathically with the question that sparked the collaboration to construct the play: "How do I authentically live inside this world?"

4

Empathic Disempowerment

Acknowledge your rejection and negation of us, to
own the fact that you stole our lands, our personhood,
our self-respect; Gringo, accept the doppelganger in
your psyche. By taking back your collective shadow
the intracultural split will heal.

PLAYING WITH THE figure of the loop, this chapter begins by analyzing an apology in which a white man kneels in a ritual of purification, much like in *Indigurrito*, but this time the event is not performance art. I will pay attention to the genre of the apology as a
performative utterance (Austin) and the role it gives its audience
(Ahmed). While the apology by Veterans Stand With Standing Rock
answers to Anzaldúa's interpellation, I also return to this interpellation as it is translated into ceramics and painting by Kukuli
Velarde. The loop serves a theoretical purpose, given that I revisit
Anzaldúa's interpellation of the white man and the demand that he
acknowledge acts of physical and psychological violence. Here, the
relationship of the body to a body of knowledge reemerges. This
will be evident in Philadelphia-based Peruvian artist Velarde's paintings and sculptures, which critically reinterpret the consequences

of colonialism while borrowing from pre-Columbian visual culture. The processes that structure our understanding of other people's experience demand rehearsals that envision different responses to tradition and its history. A connection between Native peoples and Latinx communities in the US is established by studying how two re-readings of a colonial past (of rejection and occupation common to both) wrestle with different frameworks of visibility. Empathic disempowerment entails a form of empathy that does not inspire or uplift the powerful, nor makes them feel grateful or lucky for their privileged positions; rather, is an invitation to do just the opposite, a decrease of power or a stepping down from the moral pedestal. Studying in performance the present presence of one big colonial gaze is a way of not taking whites out of the ethnic groups to be observed.

When White Men Turn Around: Clark's Space

There is a part in *Borderlands*, included at the beginning of this chapter as an epigraph, in which Anzaldúa commands white society to "acknowledge your rejection and negation of us, to own the fact that you stole our lands, our personhood, our self-respect." She continues: "Gringo, accept the doppelganger in your psyche. By taking back your collective shadow the intracultural split will heal."[1] The question then becomes what happens once this acknowledgment finally occurs. Is there healing? Who gets to heal? A great deal of attention is given to disempowered individuals who empower themselves (as in a Disney movie), but the same critical attention is not devoted to acts of disempowerment. Anzaldúa's words acknowledge the "neurosis," in Franz Fanon's terms, of the colonized and the colonizer.[2] The negative qualities attributed to minorities derive, according to her, from a need for white people to transfer the negative parts of themselves. So there is not only a double consciousness of the border, there is also the "doppelganger in the psyche of the one that discriminates against the Chicano" or any other minority.[3] In a sense, Anzaldúa proposes decolonizing the mind of the colonizer as well.

The apology at Standing Rock by Veterans Stand[4] displays the harm that colonialism produces and its collateral psychological violence. The veteran's presence was led by Wesley Clark Jr., a US Army veteran, along with Michael A. Wood Jr., a former Baltimore police officer and Marine Corps veteran. They organized the deployment that formed Veterans Stand for Standing Rock to support blocking the construction of the Dakota Access Pipeline that would carry 470,000 barrels of crude oil a day through North Dakota, South Dakota, Iowa, and Illinois, endangering the water supply and once again displacing the Lakota nation.[5] Clark himself states in an interview that he had envisioned they would simply outmaneuver the police, get across the river, and then surround the pipeline. But at the same time, he always wanted to start the protest with what the tribe calls a "Wiping the Tears Ceremony."[6] He has post-traumatic stress disorder, as do many of the other men out there with him, so he thought it was very important to "kind of spiritually cleanse us and prepare us for what I expected to be harsh tactics and beatings and jailing from the security forces."[7] Levi Rickert, publisher and editor of *Native News Online*, was there covering the events. He recalls that there was a bridge to get across the mentioned river, but it had been damaged months before, "on that night they were shooting water canons on Native Americans, pepper spraying people on the front line, so this bridge apparently got burned."[8]

What Clark refers to as a Wiping of the Tears Ceremony has been widely referred to as an apology delivered on Dec. 5, 2016. There is a video posted on YouTube from Our Revolution that shows the apology delivered by Clark, dressed in a cavalry uniform. Behind him, a group of eight to ten veterans stands. During the ceremony, Clark knelt before the elders, asking for their forgiveness for the long and systematically brutal acts of conquest:

> Many of us, me particularly, are from the units that have hurt you over many years. We came. We fought you. We took your land. We signed treaties that we broke. We stole minerals from your sacred hills. We blasted the faces of our presidents onto your sacred mountain. Then we took still more land and then we took your children and then we tried to take your language. We tried to eliminate your

language that God gave you, and the Creator gave you. We didn't
respect you, we polluted your Earth, we've hurt you in so many ways
but we've come to say that we are sorry. We are at your service and
we beg for your forgiveness.[9]

The verbs "took," "stole," "blasted," "eliminated," and the objects
"land," "children," "minerals," "sacred hills," "language" are part
of a common story in the conquest of what is now Anglo and Hispanic America.

J. L. Austin considered the apology as a particular kind of performative utterance, which he called "behabitives": "a kind of performative concerned roughly with reactions to behaviour and with
behaviour towards others; designed to exhibit attitudes and feelings."[10] Its behavior-related nature makes apparent the attitudes
and feelings an era considers appropriate to direct *toward* others.
The apology contrarily to other types of actions demands a reading
from its audience. Sara Ahmed points that, "with an apology, the
addressee also has to read the utterance. The utterance is addressed
to the other, whose gaze returns to the speaker, who is placed in
a history that precedes the utterance."[11] For Levi Rickert, the fact
that Clark was wearing a cavalry hat and blazer clearly placed the
speaker in a particular history,

> Clark organized it [the apology]; he came to us in what I would call
> a cavalry uniform. Clark's apology really kind of extended for years
> and years of war that the cavalry fought against Native Americans,
> the American Indians, and even the Great Plains during the eigh-
> teen hundreds. Yes there is some serious history that takes place
> in the Great Plains, of atrocities against native people, and there
> is no two ways about it, the 7th cavalry was trying to get away with
> native people, they were just trying to eliminate us, they wanted to
> see us disappear from the face of the earth.[12]

After Clark knelt, everyone who was non-Native and was willing
to apologize for what the US government had done to Native peoples also knelt. He removed his hat out of respect, without knowing what was to come: "I knew I should probably take my hat off. I

didn't know Crow Dog was going to lay his hand on my head. I'm glad he did. It felt wonderful. It felt healing. It felt good, in the truest sense of the word."[13] "Leonard Crow Dog, who has since passed away, was of such renown, so revered as an elder, that for him to give the blessing or hear the . . . to accept the apology was pretty significant."[14] This ritual was initially conceived in preparation for the expected harsh tactics countering the protest. The Veterans intended initially to retake the Backwater Bridge, which had been damaged since October. The violence and its ways of inhabiting the camp had many facets; so, detailed planning was not feasible, plans had to be rearranged:

> There were paid infiltrators, we believe, both in the camp and that had come into our own group, that were managed by the private security firms that work for DAPL. The view I got from the elders was that what [the infiltrators] wanted was violence at the bridge and on the front line, which they could then call a riot. We believe they had a financial incentive to make it violent, so the best thing to do was peace and prayer and keep distance from the security forces. And don't forget, by causing problems up there—and violence—and then leaving shortly after, we would have left the tribe to deal with all the ugly fallout from it.[15]

It makes sense that a person familiar with US military interventions abroad, which often leave a damaged landscape and social fabric on their way out, would think this way.[16] In a similar manner, past massacres—most notably, those at Wounded Knee in 1890 and 1973—are fresh in the memory of the Sioux Nation. In remembrance of these massacres and in light of ongoing aggressions, the tribe took a nonviolent stance that was directly communicated to people in the camps. Nicole Willis, former special assistant for Indian affairs in the US Department of Labor, and one of the panelists for *Uprising 12/13*, states that:

> Tensions with law enforcement started getting higher, and there were more nonviolent direct actions that were resulting in arrests

or violence, you know, the tribe came in and said, please don't try to get arrested, please don't try to incite violence. But there were people there who wanted that, because they thought that a greater action would cause a greater reaction . . . and the North Dakota law enforcement and private security [TigerSwan] were waiting to lose it. If you saw the footage of them, they loved it when they got to be violent and act crazy, and some people wanted to engage in that hoping that it would blow up the cause even bigger, but the tribe having to be responsible for their citizens and for people on their land did not condone that.[17]

There were moments then in which the focus was taken away from the health of the community in favor of the global struggle.[18] Veterans' bodies staged a subject position permeated by social dramas and traumas; other activists came to stage different histories and had other priorities in mind. Putting oneself on the receiving end of violence might disempower not only the self but also the person one stands in solidarity with; this is one of the conundrums in a reality informed by a cultural split. Similar to the behabitive of the apology, empathy will here go in two directions when one inhabits the shoes of the other, one in which one imagines the gaze on the other side and another in which one re-enacts the consequences, the futures, of present solidarities.

During Clark's apology, many people in the audience cried, and afterward people shook hands and embraced. Rickert, who was there covering the event and taking pictures, states that "it was a highly emotional moment, it was an emotional scene. I was trying to get a good vantage point from different angles, and it is my opinion that the apology was very well received by Native Americans. I remember some of the pictures I took there were a lot of intense looks on the faces of people. Yes, it was a very important moment, very intense."[19] The event was also an opportunity for closure, as just the day before, on December 4, 2016, the Obama administration had denied the permit for the pipeline to be built.

In a sense, the interpellation that Anzaldúa delivered in *Borderlands* was carried out in person in this intracultural encounter.

In an interview, Sara Van Gelder asked Clark about the text of the apology:

Gelder: It's interesting to hear that you didn't know what you were going to say because you listed very specific, very powerful sources of trauma and deep hardship. You listed them so eloquently and succinctly. What were you drawing from?

Clark: How could I not? On Saturday night, we had a gathering out at Sitting Bull College with about 400–500 of the vets, and tribal elders spoke. And whenever they get up to speak, they name off what's happened. They let people know, this is what happened. It was the same thing during the ceremony. Each elder who got up and spoke did it. The past is very fresh because it affects their day-to-day lives today. They are still trying to recover culturally and economically in every way.[20]

The meetings between Veterans Stand and the Lakota people are both an intercultural and an intracultural encounter, for the predominant culture is part of both parties' worlds. The split belongs to both sides. In this performance of apology, the interpellation and the reaction work differently than in Althusser's paradigm. In Louis Althusser's classic interpellative scene, the policeman shouts, "Hey you," and the turning subject reacts to the call, just to prove their innocence, even if they are not sure who "you" is.[21] In this apology there is an acknowledgment of the crimes that directly responds to Anzaldúa's command. As we learned, this derived from the constant reminders the elders raised every time they spoke in gatherings between Veterans Stand and the Lakota people.

The history preceding the apology and the present violence affects the readings of this performative utterance. The day after the Sitting Bull College gathering that Clark mentions there was a rally at Cannonball, a city five miles south of the camps at Standing Rock. Here 1,500 to 2,000 veterans got up in a circle; there were also tribal officials, including the former president of the Oglala Sioux, Bryan Brewer. In this gathering overhead drones, either from law enforcement or hired by the private security company, would fly really low and take pictures of the rally participants. On December 4, coming back from that rally, the veterans had every intention to go and open the bridge up.[22] But then two things happened, the tribal officials, including Dave Archambault II told veterans that this was a prayer camp, they did not want violence. Also, that night as everybody was trying to get in to the Center Rock Camp, and many journalists and people were listening to Cornell West's talk, journalists started getting reports that the Army Corps of Engineers rejected the permit.[23] At that time, car horns started honking, people were clapping and cheering, it was a moment of collective celebration.

Ricket explained, "The apology the next day was anticlimactic to the extent that veterans wanted to open the bridge and that did not happen that weekend."[24] Indeed, that did not happen for months. In January of 2017 the Backwater Bridge was still blocked. The Casino, where Clark's apology took place, was loosing revenue because of this blockade. Jenni Monet reported for the *Indian Country Media Network* on Jan. 31, 2017 that "[a]s a financial solution, Standing Rock is now holding out for the reopening of Highway 1806 at a river crossing known as the Backwater Bridge. Dismantling the blockade would mean, both literally and symbolically, bridging two sides that have been fiercely at odds—those who support the pipeline versus those who do not."[25] Many lengthy meetings ensued. "After all those meetings, some going past midnight, the situation hadn't seemed to change. Instead, it raised genuine questions that the Headsman [Manape LaMere] had posted on Facebook days earlier.[26] Can we make peace on that bridge? Can the bridge actually bridge gaps? Can battlegrounds become a place for healing?"[27]

Because the performance took place a day after the Obama administration denied the final approval for the pipeline, many—among them Michael Wood and Sedef Buyukataman—were discomfited by the apology. "They felt like Clark was drawing attention away from the moment, from the Standing Rock Sioux, and focusing it on himself. Later that day, Tribal Chairman Dave Archambault II ordered an estimated 14,000 protesters to go home."[28] It would have been significant, at least symbolically, if the apology had been performed before Obama's response. And, it could have

had legal potential, if the apology came from official entities belonging to the current government. As Ahmed points out, it is not only
about feelings, "the apology could become the basis of an appeal
for compensation; it could be 'taken up' as evidence of responsibility rather than feeling."[29] "In order to think about the 'trouble'
of apologies we need to explore the relation between the utterance,
feeling and action."[30] Levi Rickert also pointed out in our interview
that, in retrospect "I rather seen that Clark came and said hi this
is from the secretary of the army, I want to apologize on behalf of.
So, it is like as I am sitting here and thinking it through . . . I never
thought about . . . as much as I am right now . . . I just think . . . it
was more symbolic than being meaningful. Like I said, had he come
with a proclamation or an apology from official US Government,
in particular the US army, to me it would be as much more significant."[31] The Obama administration came as close as putting in a
document this apology, "it was buried in a Defense Budget package
legislation that went through at midnight, but Obama never went
ahead and said..."[32]

The sense of justice and victory did not last long. On January
24, 2017, President Donald Trump signed an executive order that
reversed the Obama legislation and advanced the construction of
the pipeline, expediting the environmental review. The pipeline was
built and operated until January 2021. Following a 200,000-gallon
Keystone pipeline oil spill in November 2017, Judge James Boasberg imposed several interim measures on the ongoing operation
of the Dakota Access pipeline. The tribe sued, and in March 2020,
a federal judge, James E. Boasberg, sided with them and ordered
the US Army Corps of Engineers to conduct a full environmental
impact statement. Since the environmental assessment was not carried out, the District Court for the District of Columbia ordered the
pipeline to be shut down in July 2020, but days later, on August 5,
the Court of Appeals for the District of Columbia Circuit reversed
the order, and the pipeline continued to operate. Trump applied
changes to the National Environmental Policy Act to circumvent
the need for environmental impact assessments. In the end, justice

was not reached, at least not until the Biden administration's executive order canceling the permit.

In retrospect, we can say that Wesley Clark Jr. and Michael Wood used the ideological location of their subject position as a source for this performance, much as Anzaldúa used the geographical location of her birth as a source for her theorizing. Anzaldúa's emphasis was on her own present and future consciousness: the self is as much a category of study as the other; Clark's emphasis was on his past and how an objective reading of it changes consciousness in the present. The tools of Black feminism could be employed in the service of decolonization, to work on what could be called "white realism." Patricia Collins's themes of self-definition and self-valuation can be deployed to mobilize "constructive and accurate images" of white history.[33] A holistic and historical view of subject positions helps to "challenge the process that imposes stereotypical images."[34] It helps to "replace externally derived images," because power also imposes images of the powerful on themselves.[35] Here, a self-defined standpoint provides perspective. Instead of always using the same muscle, the body of knowledge begins to grasp reality differently.

Enactments of disempowerment are rehearsals on the material reality of values put into behavior. They remap the coordinates of the self, expanding a too narrowly located identity. The apology can "confound socially prescriptive patterns"[36] in a manner that is neither oppositional nor uncritical. By representing a positionality that has been rendered unthinkable by the dominant culture, people from a military background at a protest that opposes the predatory force of capital can be read as an act of disidentification. The repositioning of the self in empathic enactments of disempowerment needs to be motivated by the well-being of others, not of the self, but the self benefits by gaining firsthand experience of how power is seen from outside.[37]

Intercultural understanding in enactments of power can lead to disidentifying with intracultural prejudices about the other. Focusing attention on enactments of disempowerment underscores another aspect of disidentification. Defying the salvific narrative of white power in history does more than produce a product. For the purposes of developing elaborative empathy skills, information is not knowledge. Information about massacres and atrocities might shock without providing avenues for developing attention (caring for) skills to act upon. On the other hand, one fact, well understood, can change a whole worldview and spark action. The quantity of information is not what matters, but rather its effect on personal behavior.

The problem of other minds and intercultural understanding discussed in regard to *¡Bienvenidos Blancos!* could apply to this performance as well. Its reception shows that caring for others—assuming people in Veterans Stand do care—does not always result in congratulations. After stepping down from a pedestal to see reality at the surface level, one often encounters reactions that echo mistrust and misunderstanding. The burden of representing an identity, so familiar to minorities in our America, reappears in this still-intercultural scenario. For many, the spiritual aspect of the apology ritual might resonate with Anzaldúa's notion of nepantla. *Nepantla* means "in-between space" in Nahuatl; it acknowledges the psychic violence following shifts in consciousness that try to find meaning from chaos, and it seeks to avoid the romanticization of borderlands that sometimes ensued in the realm of theory.[38] Inhabiting thresholds is not easy. Blows could come from all fronts. Empathic disempowerment can be criticized as incomplete, inefficient, fake, sloppy: caring has a non-heroic side. To understand less powerful others, in an egalitarian form of engagement that works in their service, the self has to be open to the possibility of being misunderstood. One of the most important aspects of intercultural relations is whom they do indeed benefit, and how different parties benefit from it. So it is not an illogical concern to expect efficiency; it is just that this adds a new moral level of vulnerability. Failing to take empathetic action means there is nothing to be explained: being part of something society tells us "is not our place," however, creates a dislocation of expectations that affects the psychic limits of elaborative empathy.[39] The psychic limits refer to the 'what', 'where', 'who,' and 'why' that inform the images, emotional memories and motives of 'moving the self' while expanding emotional borderlands.

Returning to Anzaldúa's interpellation of the "gringo," once the "gringo" "acknowledges," it is not clear whether the gesture will be accepted wholeheartedly. Exploring this response to enactments of disempowerment is important for understanding elaborative empathy. That a white man delivered the apology at the pipeline protest was the whole point of the performance, yet it met skepticism from across the political spectrum. When the white man turns around to acknowledge the interpellative call, the double consciousness of decolonizing the mind generates two tracks of responses: what peers see (that is, in-group reception of foreign behavior) and what others see (that is, reception by members of the out-group). Perhaps in the military, as a former Navy Seal expressed in an episode of *This American Life*, empathy is more a liability than a skill: "The military trains you to separate emotion from the mission . . . you lose a degree of empathy in the military because empathy is not an advantageous skill to have. Empathy is not a useful emotion to have."[40] Yet, here were the members of Veterans Stand, showing empathy and expressing emotions. And still, this ceremony put the subaltern in the position, once again, of delivering healing, performing emotional labor for those in the dominant group.

The presence and apology of Veterans Stand put people with a military background on both sides of the protest over the construction of the Dakota Access Pipeline. Veterans enacting an apology, showing vulnerability, and admitting wrongdoing departs from the American dream of pure intentions and strong efforts. It also departs from the zero-sum game of actions achieve change or they are worth nothing, possibly being seen as merely aesthetic or in the best-case scenario, as purely ameliorative. Eve Sedgwick vindicates the possible restorative outcomes to consider, while fighting back against this revolution or nothing approach,

> Reparative motives, once they become explicit are inadmissible in paranoid theory [one that centers around the process of false

consciousness and takes suspicion as a methodology inherent to critical practice] both because they are about pleasure ("merely aesthetic") and because they are ameliorative ("merely reformist"). What makes pleasure and amelioration so "mere"? Only the exclusiveness of paranoia's faith in demystifying exposure: only its cruel and contemptuous assumption that the one thing lacking for global revolution, explosion of gender roles, or whatever, is people's (that is, other people's) having the painful effects of their oppression, poverty, or deludedness sufficiently exacerbated to make the pain conscious (as if otherwise it wouldn't have been) and intolerable (as if intolerable situations were famous for generating excellent solutions).[41]

Sedgwick is here concerned with rescuing other types of hermeneutics beyond the hermeneutics of "suspicion and its concomitant privileging of paranoia."[42] She did not discard this type of theorization but thought that it should be "viewed as one kind of cognitive/affective theoretical practice among other, alternative kinds."[43] As I mentioned earlier, the addressee's response is a constitutive element of the apology, but the expectations expressed by Clark were of personal healing, the motives were reparative, although it is not clear how much healing was considered on the side of the Lakota people. We know one of their members at the Oceti Sakowin Headsman Council reflected on whether battlegrounds can become a place for healing.[44] Because of the legacy and renown of Crow Dog, Rickert states that he was glad he was there, whether or not he can really speak of the true intent of Clark. The "we are at your service" part of the apology seems to promise some future actions, and there were rumors that Clark had made promises, to go to Flint in Michigan, even work with some tribes there for water protection.[45] Rickert continues, "I don't want to be disrespectful of the process because I do believe . . . it would be my opinion that Crow Dog took him on his word and accepted the apology."[46] This in no way cancels the value of the apology; on the contrary, it only highlights the power dynamics at play. Since power dynamics could never be erased, it is healthy and honest to at least inquire about them. What do these veteran subjects gain and lose in the societies to which they belong by these types of acts? Can we judge the elders' acceptance of this apology as if we know better? What authorizes us to do so?

On the Spectacle of Empathy

The doubt surrounding the Veterans Stand event focused on whether it was a hoax, not on the feelings of the Lakota nation's chief and/or the Lakota people. The world of art is concerned with disempowered subjects that empower themselves—that is, the happy ending—but is reluctant to consider powerful subjects that disempower themselves. There are several reasons for this reluctance. First, there is a long history of faking good intentions and contrition. Second, there is no need to put oneself at risk of believing. And third, if we see any value in the actions taken by a subject identified with power, we risk closing the gap between power and ourselves: many times, very little stands between the position of power and our own position. "Calling in," (instead of calling out) as University of Pennsylvania communications specialist, professor, and activist Jessa Lingel notes, demands an active sorting out of values, requires tons of energy, and takes away the hierarchical structure that often calling out establishes.[47] Considering the possibility of good intentions is read as a sign of complicity with power and, most importantly, as falling prey to either ideology or credulity. Scandals about the use of funds raised for Veterans Stand following the apology depict the material reality of this mistrust. In this realm, accountability is one way in which this trust in empathic thought could be regained or proved to be worthy. Giving account methodically of who is benefiting economically from activists' anti-colonial efforts might be a simple but objective way of assessing endeavors. This is crucial since memories of scandals affect future collaborations and might even obstruct empathy, as the higher-order goal of not being cheated will overrule the possibility of participatory empathy.

On the other hand, this mistrust is legitimate, as it is calling out spectacles of empathy. Being accountable is crucial for reenvisioning relations in our America. For example, we saw an explosion of face-saving efforts and "powerful statements" in response to George Floyd's killing in 2020. For many businesses, it became a public relations necessity to express sympathy with the Black Lives Matter (BLM) movement. Mehrsa Baradan's account of and response to one of these performances, on the National Public Radio show *1A*, makes clear that there are moments in which action needs to follow empathy; otherwise, it is pure spectacle.[48] Empathy acts in the service of the self rather than of the other when performed to avoid the disempowerment of the powerful. Here is Baradan's response:

> I think one of the most salient images of this corporate action [a public image showing solidarity for Black Lives matter and/or apologizing] was Jamie Dimon kneeling in front of Chase Manhattan or Chase Bank. You don't have to go back as far as slavery to see what Chase has done. You go back to the subprime crisis in 2008 and look at the areas that were targeted with these loans that saw . . . the Black community lost 53 percent of their wealth during the subprime crisis, and a lot of these banks, when they got bailed out, were supposed to modify these mortgages, which is to save the homeowners. What they did instead was foreclose on their homes. So, my response to that was why don't you get off your knees, go back inside, and give people back their homes. So stop kneeling and doing this sort of imaging and do the actual stuff.[49]

In the equation that privileges begging for forgiveness instead of asking for permission, asking for permission (a sign of respect) is only valued when it can help to avoid being sued.[50] Otherwise, the loophole of forgiveness (one response to repentance) leaves the damaged parties with both the damage and the emotional labor of their response. Clark's performance of an apology is a paradigmatic example of this transaction. I did not discard the possibility of real, personal, individual interests not in tune with empathic thought, but my interest lies in the apology's reception. To attribute value to the apology delivered by Clark and the other members of Veterans Stand was seen by many as falling for another self-promotion and/or face-saving effort in which, as so often happens, no action follows. The varied receptions of this performance help rethink the gap between performances of empowerment and performances of disempowerment.

The violence accompanying contact zones in our America ensures that actions purporting to demonstrate disempowerment are likely to be mistrusted or misunderstood in a culture where it is easier to express contrition than give up profits. In this case, elaborative empathy can only serve to give the benefit of the doubt to possible good intentions, and to the eventuality of good outcomes. In the broader American culture, empathy could be disempowering. Heather Havrilesky, the advice columnist for *New York Magazine*, notes:

> If you do a deep dive into American culture, there is a lot of cutthroat competition for resources and survival of the fittest, a sort of belief in that you can either make it or you can fall into the gutter. And you know what happens to you is never a matter of best circumstances or unfortunate situations, it is all sort of like, "Did you, were you victorious? Did you climb to the top of the heap, or were you some kind of loser who can't win?" Winning and losing is such a recurring theme in our culture. There's kind of been a turn in which we are cynical; we have gone from valuing kindness to valuing the sound of kindness, sort of like when a tragedy happens and all the politicians go online and say, "Our thoughts and prayers are with this person." Because of the way social media works . . . we come to see thoughts and prayers themselves as a cliché that means nothing.[51]

This performance plays with all those variables. The apology came in place of taking the bridge, an action more in tune with "winning." It is clear that the bridge was more than a physical space. Clark mentioned the feeling of healing in regard to this ceremony where the apology took center stage. Likewise, one of the tribal officials, Manape LaMere, reflected on whether the battleground at Backwater Bridge could be a place of healing, and on whether the bridge could bridge the gap.[52] Giving up a bridge, taking a bridge, using the bridge (at that time, fenced with security wire and jersey barriers) to bridge gaps where all part of the emotional landscape in this cold and snowy season of protests.

When White Men Turn Around

To account for the psychic borderlands in the communities of the powerful, one should try to understand what is disempowering for them. Only then can empathic enactments of disempowerment be given full attention. The empathic disempowerment proposed by Clark's performance responds to Anzaldúa's interpellation but at the same time highlights the challenges occurring once acknowledgment is achieved. This performance briefly portrayed the grid of intelligibility that hegemonic traditions obliterate, but the relationality advanced fell short when once again the ritual staged a white subject "confessing" self-reflexivity and the colonized or racialized subject as the occasion for self-reflexivity.[53] This could also be seen as part of the psychic borderlands in the communities of the powerful. I here close the first loop I presented at the beginning, the mirroring white confessing subjects kneeling in an act of apology in two performances that reflect on the American experience of otherness.

WHEN THE GAZE RECEIVES A "RETURN TO SENDER"

There is a second loop, which I drew between Anzaldúa's textual interpellation and Peruvian-born, Philadelphia-based artist Kukuli Velarde. Kukuli Velarde's practice spans ceramic sculpture and painting, drawing deeply on her cultural heritage. The artist's figures, which often take the form of imagined entities, layer self-portraiture with references to the ancient pottery of Peru, directly connecting with larger issues of gender and the effects of colonization on her home country. Born in Cuzco, Peru, and now a resident of the South Kensington neighborhood of Philadelphia for more than two decades, Velarde studied at Hunter College, City University of New York, and was an artist in residence at The Clay Studio from

1997 to 2001. The artist's work is present in museum collections including the New Taipei City Yingge Ceramics Museum in Taiwan, the Pennsylvania Academy of Fine Arts, and the Museum of Fine Arts in Houston. Her first US solo exhibition of her paintings took place at Taller Puertorriqueño in 2018. She received a Guggenheim Fellowship in 2015, and her work was included in New Grit: Art & Philly Now, a major exhibition at the Philadelphia Museum of Art.[54]

Through the visual arts, Kukuli delivered Anzaldúa's interpellation by challenging the body of knowledge that makes the body intelligible. She proposes a form of empathic disempowerment that focuses on the epistemic violence of aesthetic traditions. Her aesthetics point to social transformation by disempowering the hegemonic gaze, but at the same time, empower other ways of looking.

Kukuli's work could be read as a visual narrative that translates Anzaldúa's interpellation into art. The outrage Kukuli felt about the celebration in New York of the five hundredth anniversary of Columbus's landing in the Caribbean moved her to create her first solo show, which, like *Indigurrito*, was performed in 1992: "It was an opportunity because at that time, we had this five hundredth anniversary of Columbus landing, and I thought that it was actually outrageous that we were actually thinking that that celebration was something that should be done, when it meant the death of millions and millions of people.[55] So I felt so outraged and I needed to do something, and what I did was, I just went with my pieces, with my babies, I made these babies."[56] *We, the Colonized Ones* represents babies that were never born; they never had the opportunity to come to life because of history.[57] Kukuli had been painting since childhood, but she felt at that time that "paintings didn't have a connection to my soul."[58] As Kukuli worked in a ceramics studio as part of her BFA at Hunter College, she was confronted with an issue that moved her spirit, frustrations, and passions. *We, the Colonized Ones* was the result. These ceramic babies were produced without glaze because, Kukuli explained, "glaze was a creation brought by the conquistadors."[59] Each piece represents or symbolizes the emotional consequences of European colonization: every piece is like a scream, every piece is emotional work.[60] One of the first pieces

FIGURE 4.1 *Daddy Likee?* Painting by Kukuli Velarde; photo by Gustavo García, Colibrí Workshop. ©Taller Puertorriqueño. All rights reserved.

in the series was a cross that hung from a window near Columbus Circle. Kukuli expected that "all those who parade by Broadway near Columbus Circle [would] see it."[61] That parallels the 2020 BLM protests that questioned the value of maintaining certain monuments and statues (among them, those of Columbus). Kukuli was calling for the participants in a parade created to bring pride to the Italian American community to disempower this colonization-based pride. She clarified at that time, "The white man I am going against is the one that lives inside us"[62] She felt called to engage in an ongoing struggle: "I have a mission to talk about what I see, what I feel, and what I am going through, because colonization has not ended."[63]

Like Nao Bustamante, Kukuli is performing as herself, and she is doing so not only as an individual but as a cultural and historical result. After having a baby, Kukuli stopped the unborn babies series; the babies now have her daughter's face, much like the ceramics in the series *Plunder Me Baby*, which all have Kukuli's face. As we will see, *Plunder Me Baby* contrasts with her newer work, *A Mi Vida,* named after her child, Vida, born when Kukuli was forty-eight years old. *A Mi Vida*'s artistic proposal affirms that it embraces babies in danger because of the Trump administration's policies on family separation for immigrants, particularly those from Central America.

Kukuli's first solo exhibition of paintings in the United States, *The Complicit Eye*, was accompanied by a participatory performance that took place at the gallery on its opening night where the audience had to hold a large, heavy ceramic sculpture, *A mi Vida I*. The heavy weight of the "baby" assured that no participant "forgot" to pass it around. This, in turn, created a network of relations among the viewers of the paintings hanging in the very same gallery. Kukuli walked around to different groups, explaining, responding to questions, or simply engaging with the viewers. The participatory performance that was part of the opening weeks of *The Complicit Eye* adds different layers of "struggle with a 'story' (concept or theory) embracing personal and social identity; they also show how this 'embrace' is a *bodily* activity."⁶⁴

Kukuli said in 1996 that her images come from indigenous aesthetics, which is evident in both her ceramics and her paintings. In her painting *Daddy Likee?*, she put this visual culture onto the canvas through the use of space. Kukuli asserts that transitional Incan textiles, those produced in the first decades of the Spanish conquest and thus adapting to shifting cultural paradigms, inspired the painting's background. Judging from the presence of geometric and figurative forms, we can assume the textiles are *cumbis*, high-quality cloth used by Incan nobility and elites. The designs are called *tocapus*. "Tocapus are small quadrangles filled with geometric or stylized figurative motifs that appear in series on textiles and ceremonial goblets of the Inca and Early Colonial Periods."⁶⁵ Silverman shows that, "later, figures began to act as *tocapus* as well, floating along the fabric."⁶⁶ In this period, "warp-patterning textiles and tapestries began to gain predominance, a curious interplay arose between the two traditions. *Tocapus* and other small-scale geometric elements were woven in both methods, while figurative elements and, occasionally, alphabetic writing found their way into the warp-patterned weaving lexicon."⁶⁷ The designs are part of the artistic wealth from a period in which textiles began to integrate Western elements as a result of the cultural, social, and economic hecatomb brought by the conquest.

Kukuli reflects this *mestizaje* through the elements of the textile. She explores the imposition of aesthetics that invalidated native aesthetics, causing a crisis in the understanding of the self. This crisis is the organizing concept for *The Complicit Eye*. The artist comments that a Google search sparked her interest in the relationship between beauty and a colonial past in the present: when she googled "Peruvian faces," the results included pages on the ugliest Latin American faces. She wanted to highlight the fact that this connection between indigeneity and ugliness belongs to a past that lives in the present, where whiteness is beauty. Violence and exploitation fall disproportionately on those deemed "ugly."

Empathic disempowerment here comes by way of rebuffing the hegemonic aesthetics of beauty and embracing that which oppressive cultural norms reject in order to create another grid of intelligibility for relations. On a side note, this empathic disempowerment is voluntary, as it is in the case of demonstrators being repressed in peaceful BLM protests. However, involuntary disempowerment might also prove transformational, as in the case of US senators who found themselves for the first time on the losing end of white supremacy during the insurrection that perturbed the white space of Congress in January 2021.[68] The difference between one and the other is that in the former, the disempowerment is occasioned by an empathic impetus, but in the latter, the experience of disempowerment opens the gates for empathy.

Empathy and Aesthetics

The aesthetic history of empathy fosters reflection on the nature of Kukuli's interpellative works of art. As I mentioned in the introduction, the term was coined as a translation of the German Einfühlung to denote an emotion associated with understanding works of art.[69] The word *empathy* emerged from German aesthetics, but an aesthetic use of the term continued during the twentieth century in

Anglo-American philosophy. Work by Vernon Lee (aka Violet Paget) on psychological aesthetics brought further attention to empathy. For her, empathy was "the tendency to merge the *activities* of the perceiving subject with the qualities of the perceived object," which ensures that action is only in the hands of one subject.[70] Empathy, she explained, could be found "in all modes of speech and thought"; for that reason, it "still helps us to many valuable analogies; and it is possible that without its constantly checked but constantly renewed action, human thought would be without logical cogency, as it certainly would be without poetical charm."[71] These valuable analogies that might assure logical cogency are one of the great contributions of art. Lee observes that "the contemplation of beautiful shapes," which she later explains could be also ideas, traits, and the like, "involves perceptive processes, in themselves mentally invigorating and refining, and a play of empathic feelings, which realize the greatest desiderata of spiritual life."[72] Importantly, "such perceptive and empathic activities cannot fail to raise the present level of existence and to leave behind a higher standard for future experience."[73] The aesthetic experience connects perceptive activities to intellectual and emotional life at once; here empathy is "lifted" by beauty just as much as by perception. Moreover, empathy connects to spiritual life via aesthetics.

To make clearer what empathy is, Lee clarifies what it is not. Two misinterpretations she observes are of interest here. The first one consists of believing that the aesthetic take on empathy belongs to a projection of the ego onto the object. For Lee, there cannot be a projection of the ego because empathy merges activities of the perceiving subject with the qualities of the perceived object, which actually depends on the "momentary abeyance of all thought of an ego."[74] Nor is empathy an animation of the inanimate.[75] The animation we are aware of is "going on *in us*."[76] This connection to inner activity could be controversial if, instead of aesthetic objects, we speak of people and experience. Just to be clear, that was not Lee's intent. She once noted, "my aesthetics will always be those of the gallery and the studio, and not of the laboratory."[77] Yet when we speak of performance, these two forms of experience at times mingle.

In the Anglo-American philosophical arena, an Oxford-based group was particularly concerned with "solving" the problem of beauty;[78] I believe their reflections shed light on the problem of empathy. The initial problem, quite expected, was to determine whether beauty lay in the object or in the eye of the beholder. This is a concern that *The Complicit Eye* echoes. In philosophical terms, this translated to a tension between a property of the object and a judgment of taste as subjective state.[79] It was of utmost importance to this school of thought "how the object brought about feelings in the observer, and the observer then wholly identified with the object:"[80] "The experience of beauty is an experience of utter union with the object; every barrier is broken down, and the beholder feels that his own soul is living in the object, and that the object is unfolding its life in his own heart."[81] This experience of the 'object' of beauty seems almost a process of fetishization[82]; Lee considered it a mythologization.

I draw heavily on this aesthetic take on empathy—the original empathy!—to draw attention to how the "object" sometimes resembles minorities in a state of ethnographic entrapment, "when peoples are not producers of thought and analysis [but] rather they are ethnographically entrapped as mascots of social and political movements."[83] Elaborative empathy brings to the fore the conditions and contexts of other people's situations. It is then crucial to account for this tension between objective properties and subjective judgment. "The aesthetic doctrine of empathy, in which observers gave objects life by a process of total identification of the ego, was later replaced,"[84] but it is important to know about the originally unique ego that gave the observer the first move in this game of inner thoughts. For Lee, there was no identification of the ego because it was momentarily suspended, but male theorists would not suspend the presence of the ego, not even in their theoretical constructions.

In the visual arts and in narrative, this unilateral narrow empathy still prevails, and according to many critics, it has an "important role in improving our empathic skills," as we have discussed in previous chapters.[85] For Dominic McIver Lopes, distinguished professor of philosophy at the University of British Columbia and chair (until 2023) of the Board of Officers of the American Philosophical

Association, the visual arts have a couple of important differences as they relate to the rehearsal of empathic skills. First, something that is more characteristic of art is that their scenes express emotion. We know that Kukuli, for example, considers her works to be emotional labor. Emotional scenes like Kukuli's sometimes point out to the viewer whether they merit a response and how strong that response should be. In doing so, they "can play a referencing role, marking features of situations as warranting responses. The cognitive pay-off is that we learn to recognize situations as warranting certain responses, even when the expressive element is removed."[86] That is, social referencing can be trained pictorially, and it can be criticized through visual media as well. Lee noted this as well when she reaffirmed that, "for space perception and empathy and their capacity to be felt as satisfactory or unsatisfactory, the aesthetic imperative is not only intelligible but inevitable."[87] A sharp question—one so relevant to our study that it is hard to believe it was posed more than a century ago—acts as the corollary: "Instead therefore of asking: Why is there a preference for what we call Beauty? We should have to ask why has perception, feeling, logic, imagination, come to be just what it is?"[88] Kukuli's paintings in *The Complicit Eye* perform by posing, "figuratively," never better said, the questions about beauty Lee advanced.

The Complicit Eye in Performance

The Complicit Eye show was presented as "performative self-portraits that draw attention to the ways in which we are complicit in the production and promulgation of ideas about femininity and beauty—which have a very real effect on the lives of women."[89] It is clear that the words *performance* and *performative* here refer to the effects, the realities that are opened and closed, some of which are explained in the press release for the exhibition: "Velarde's drawing performance is about more than creating a composition; it is about creating connections with people."[90] The show centers on a notion of complicity that resembles Muñoz's disidentification when it is described as "a complex give and take of acceptance and resistance."[91] It is important for Kukuli to dissect the reality of female objectification and the connections between beauty and violence, these are more nuanced in *The Complicit Eye* than in *Plunder Me Baby*, which I discuss further on. The paintings in *The Complicit Eye* objectify the objectification, dissecting its standards of beauty. The more trained the eye is on Western standards of beauty advanced by renowned classical painters, the more it will perceive which crucial points of composition have been adjusted. In this way, Kukuli "critically engage[s] ways of seeing, specifically perspectivalism, which has inscribed women as given to be seen but not as given to see."[92] Thinking of sources as performance implies thinking that the contents of their messages also depend on the capacity, the experience, and the level of effort that the spectator is willing to employ in order to comprehend the artist. Nobody in a regular audience sees the same play, and the same happens with the viewers of a painting, a drawing, or a sculpture. Performance in this case acknowledges the identification of more than one ego.

The heavy ceramic baby used at the gallery opening in 2018 was part of what would later be a new performance called *A Mi Vida*. Kukuli was working on it at the time of our interview in 2021 and, because of the pandemic, it ended up happening on June 4, 2022 at the Clay Studio in North Philadelphia. The performance of *A Mi Vida*, involved seven "babies" in strollers. Sharing the exhibition with two other artists, Kukuli's corner at the front of the gallery held strollers with a ceramic baby inside each one. When Kukuli finally entered with the eighth stroller, the performative aspect of offering the babies to be held by the audience began. Kukuli would pick up each baby (all of them have the face of Kukuli's seven-year-old child, but some have animal features looking like a bird or a fish), and she passed each one around to the public. The pieces represent children incarcerated or separated from their parents because of "the immigration policies of this country at this moment."[93] In the performance for *The Complicit Eye*, Kukuli expressed that doing these ceramic babies (A mi Vida I was the only one employed that night) "was a way of prolonging the sensation of holding her daughter, Vida, in her arms, as a baby." After the shooting in Uvalde the artistic statement noted that *A*

FIGURE 4.2 Ceramic baby in the arms of an audience member at opening night of *The Complicit Eye*. Photo Senia Lopez. ©Taller Puertorriqueño. All rights reserved.

mi Vida began as a way for the artist to prolong the feeling of holding her now "elementary school-age daughter, Vida, in her arms, as a baby."[94] Four of the pieces shown on *Making Place Matter* were crafted in 2020. Kukuli specifies:

> I like the idea of breaking the separation of the audience with the object. The object is supposed to be revered, and indeed you should be really responsible not to break it. But I like the idea of people being able to hold it. First, as an approachable art piece. And second, I want the piece to symbolize the children who I am asking you to protect, as an immigrant. If I were in the situation in which I am separated from my child, I cannot imagine anything more horrific and cruel. So in the performance, the wish is to give that baby to somebody to help me protect it.[95]

The election of the material, ceramic, reinforces the idea of breakability, establishing a parallel between pieces and lives. Initially, Kukuli was thinking of having ten women (many originally from

Central America)—who would pass the ceramic pieces around for people from the audience to hold for a minute, then take them back, continue walking, and then give them to somebody else while we hear a common Spanish-language lullaby: "Duermete niño, duermete ya, que viene el cuco y te comerá and police sirens." The lullaby was heard but in the end only Kukuli passed the babies. The presence of two handheld, professional television studio cameras plus the usual iPhone recording made any engagement appear as being casted in a live TV show, rather than freely participating in a communal performance. Agreeing to hold one entailed being part of a video posted online later. Nowadays, it seems to be taken for granted that any participation will be broadcasted and no consent is needed. No man was ever offered or consented to holding one of the babies. The dynamics of interaction at this mini performance showed how "the performer make[s] apparent the ways in which bodies are stages for social theatrics; propping hosts of cultural assumptions."[96] After five minutes, six minutes, the performance ended when Kukuli put all the babies back in their strollers and left pushing one of them, leaving the other seven in place.

Kukuli's ceramic pieces are heavy because of the material, but she adds, "I like the symbolism even of the weight because to take care of a child is not a light thing to do, and asking you to carry—I don't like to use the word my burden—but, you know, to help me to carry this precious burden that is all that I have in my life as a mother, and, you know, because we are in danger."[97] Kukuli's use of babies goes hand in hand with the theme of motherhood. Motherhood is a topic with potential political capital to both conservative and progressive audiences. This political capital is often invoked through empathy. On the one hand, this overlapping between caring for others and motherhood could be read as problematic. On the other, by linking motherhood to the representation of a social issue, this gives it a social progressive edge that is, nonetheless, graspable from a conservative understanding of social issues. The same happened with her first pieces of babies that were never born, because of the conquest . . . not abortion. In this first attempt a conservative rhetoric was reworked to criticize the colonial enterprise. The fragile, heavy ceramic babies employed as if in a choreographed dance are an innovative, performative take on objects usually on pedestals within vitrines and housed in museums. In addition to putting the participating audience in the shoes of a mother, it adds the face of her own child to encourage the spectator to imagine seeing their own familiar, beloved faces as targets of the violence inflicted by a community, culture, or government. Often it is said that empathy is about putting yourself in the shoes of others, her approach here certainly imagines this scenario, but Kukuli seems to have also asked us to imagine a path of violence directed at the self while putting a familiar face in it.

Daddy Likee?

Daddy Likee? is a painting that translates Anzaldúa's interpellation into the visual arts. This painting could also be deemed an *autohistoria*. Anzaldúa talks about *autohistorias* as self-referential art that goes beyond the pictorial, that deals with both the storyteller and the stories and histories in order to best tell the story of the artist's culture.[98] All the paintings in Kukuli's exhibition seem to scream her desire to "[invent] our history from our experience and perspective through our art rather than accepting the dominant culture."[99] In the gallery at Taller Puertorriqueño's exhibition, *Daddy Likee?* took center stage, positioned directly across from the entrance. In the self-portrait, which is made on Amazonian tree bark, the artist is nude, looking straight at the viewer and surrounded by lines of text:

> Oye qué miras? Daddy Likee? Arriba arriba señorita una sonrisita? Vete a chingarte conche tu mother F. No carajo! Daddy Manan Likee? Who cares [upper border]
> Bien peruanito no? Folklórico si pués autóctono y salvaje. Bien kitch. Cholaso resentidón exótico bruit cute I love no references primitive "Latin American Art righ . . . [lower border]

Above and below these two lines of text run four other lines of text, without doubt *autohistorias* in Anzaldúa's sense, that respond to a hypothetical interlocutor:

Recuerdo de niña las miradas invasoras, tasando. El miedo a la calle.
Y las telenovelas, repitiendo la historia del príncipe azul, el rico que
se enamora de la criada, y ella lo ama aunque la viole y después de
humillaciones se casan y son dichosos. Soy virgen, dije, quieres
una veladora? dijiste . . . la inocencia del amor ignorante [telello-
ronas] te has ido.[100]

Ya estoy vieja y aun me da miedo hombres parados en la calle.
La edad me ha liberado, pero como le enseño a mi nena que todos,
todas somos iguales? Que puede ser Spider Man or Tinker Bell en
todos los Halloween de su vida? que su cuerpo es suyo y su mente
es suya, y las calles son suyas, que nadie le asuste, que nadie le haga
sentirse vulnerable jama[s]

No me digas que soy articulate, no me digas que mi acento
es cute mientras me hablas lento . . . I am as ethnic as you are.
Yo hablo Español, and English. Spokeo ambos pero mi inglés
tiene acento. Porque? Despúes de 30 años . . . nunca traté, never
wanted, never cared. Puedo ser yo sin tener que ser tú? Sin verme
como tu? Sin necesitar creerme como tú. May I be myself y no
tu remedo?

Where are you from? I know I know I am American too but where
are you really from? Germany? English? Perhaps? You are Euro-
American right? Ya pues, en serio you too came from somewhere.
I am exotic to you? You are exotic to me. Colonization, modernity,
coloniality, capitalism, neoliberalism, and here we are, looking at
each other from and within our pluriverse.

The text transitions from a past memory whose language is exclusively Spanish, to the third one that breathes in Spanglish, and then
the last one, which interpellates in what is mostly English. The first
two lines of text mark a time between childhood and late adulthood,
exposing a history of violence on the female body that even today
delimits the narrator's psychological borderlands.

The text inside the painting makes explicit a desire to "explicate
bodies in social relation."[101] This voice intends to create a new set
of gazes and expectations surrounding her daughter's bodily experiences of gender. The last two lines deal with the condescending

exotification of others in an America that simultaneously demands complete assimilation. Here the artist expresses ideas about the use of language and is unapologetic about her "accented" English after all these years in the United States. There is a direct, combative attitude about the demand to master English.

We can begin to realize that the text—there are roughly 509 words in this painting—distributes the compositional space, a sort of geometrical positionality of themes. Here Kukuli's inspiration from Incan textiles begins to open the sense of the painting.[102] She expressed that the background was inspired by one of these textiles, and it is clear that the background is not recreating the textile, but following its way of arranging the compositional space. The text in *Daddy Likee?* creates these series as much as other pictorial elements do, although its content, without a doubt, has much to say in the overall composition. In the Incan textiles, there could be many panels made of horizontal lines in two colors. Some garments, such as *uncus* used by men, were divided in three panels with the upper and lower parts in different colors and two or three lines of *tocapus* around the waistline.[103] Seventeenth- and eighteenth-century garments for women could also have horizontal lines very similar to Kukuli's background.[104]

The figures and shapes were part of a system of knowledge, originally related to a highly advanced, complex agricultural technology. The iconography not only functions to decorate a garment or fabric; it was the medium employed at the time to fix Incan wisdom.[105] Besides their practical uses, Incan textiles had a highly symbolic, hierarchical, and identitarian function.[106] During the Incan Empire, textiles also marked the regional identity of the wearer, who was obliged to wear their community's style of dress. Leaving the bodies of subjugated enemies naked was a major form of humiliation because to deprive them of their garments was to strip away their identity or to erase its presence.[107] "Warp-patterning eventually outlasted the imperial *cumbi* tradition," but "textiles remain essential manifestations and expressions of the ever-evolving identities and traditions of the Andean peoples."[108] Kukuli speaks with all the cultural resources she has at hand.

When Kukuli positions her self-portrait within this rectangular textile-like background, it is not hard to imagine a sense of royal heritage. These high-quality textiles were "a form of highly hand-crafted garment reserved for the elites."[109] Through her use of that background, she reaffirms both the nonwestern self and the status that can be claimed inside this space. The colors she employs are based on natural pigments, red being one of the first pigments employed in rituals. While the background in this painting cannot be considered homologous to a *cumbi*, it certainly retains the latter's performative spirit, especially because Kukuli wanted to work with a transitional Incan textile, and "the textiles with tocapus continued to be made and dressed by the descendants of the Inca nobility until the eighteenth century, as can be seen in the painting of the Cuzqueña School of that period."[110] Here the connection to a tradition multiplies, as tocapus were present in the Cuzco school of painting, with which Kukuli is very familiar, having painted since childhood and trained in Cuzco. Her choice of the tree bark, then, is not surprising. It was given to the artist by Christian Bendayan, a Peruvian painter from Iquitos who directs the Bufeo program, which highlights and supports Amazonian artists. This bark is used in Amazonian communities for ornamentation or dress:

> The bark on which Kukuli painted is known in the Peruvian Amazon as llanchama. It is a kind of natural fabric that is extracted from some species of trees and is prepared with blows from the blunt spine of a machete, to stretch it and "iron" it. This natural fabric used to be used to make traditional clothing, as well as to create masks that were used in the festivals of various peoples such as the Huitoto-Murui, Bora, Harankbut, and others. Several artists from this region paint their paintings on llanchama; it is a practice that has become more common since the 1990s, and today it has become a signature material for the work of some Amazonian artists.[111]

So, Kukuli is using a material that acts as the equivalent of Incan textiles in another community whose cultural heritage was decimated and is currently at risk of disappearing.

It is clear that, "who determines the *explication* of [the] body, what and how it *means*—has repeatedly been a matter of political and juridical concern"; Kukuli puts into words in *Daddy Likee*, the lived experience of these *concerns*.[112] Some additional text surrounds the small figures of women dispersed in the stripes that run above and below the sets of three lines of text, positioned in the top and bottom borders of the painting. Here again the themes of beauty, colonialism, and expectations resurface. Around the figures in the upper stripe we read the following:

> Dime como hacer para gustarte
> Vida
> Love me Diosito love me
> 48 y embarazada nunca más bella
> endrando [? ?] panza civilizandome[113]
> la raza civilizada me
> 48 embarazada nunca más bella
> Love me diosito love me
> Vida
> Dime como hacer para gustarte

Around the figures in the bottom stripe we see:

> Dime como soy para gustarme
> Love me diosito love me
> 48 y embarazada nunca más bella
> Mejorando la raza civilizandome
> Mejorando la raza civilizandome?
> 48 y embarazada nunca más bella
> Love me diosito love
> Vida
> Dime como ser para gustarte

And there is even more text, forming a central blue stripe, with text to the left and right of Kukuli's body:

Superuvian Kant. Superuvian soy. I am superuvian. If I don't criticize, if I don't burn a flag, if I don't have an abortion, I can call
myself a free individual if I reply with a nice smile when I am called
sweetie by a stranger

   If I deny where I come from, which language I speak. If I do not
look at the beggar in the train, at the black segregated in the restau-
rant, [left of body]

   at my people assimilated, alienated. If I play the game, woman
and Latina here, in the states, nice and quiet, harmless and obedi-
ent, subordinated and ignorant, I can consider myself a free individual. KV. MCMXCII (1992) [right of body]

Superuvian is a version of a Peruvian superhero, and, like all her
other self-portraits, it has Kukuli's face. Texts, again, serve as different forms of interpellation. The first plays with responses to gender expectations and harassment. It ends by providing a solution,
so to speak, stating that it should not matter if "Daddy likee." The
lower part of this text moves from gender expectations and violence to identity expectations and impositions in the world of art.
It confronts the idea of Latin American sexiness and excess, as
well as the notion that Latin American art, if it is to be considered
"real" autochthonous art by curators in the United States, must be
always "raw," folkloric, and primitive. In the middle, surrounding
Kukuli's own body, the text questions assumptions about liberty,
talking back with ironic remarks about the conditions of possibility
for the free individual. She directly confronts the game when she
explains that being free demands that she be subservient and ignorant, nice and quiet. While the text in Spanish shares common cultural expectations and norms, the English text calls out the narrow
space of freedom that assures her identity a slot at the table of representation. The last piece of text questions the position assigned
to Latinas in America. The text ends with a date coinciding with the
date of her first series of works, *Nosotros los colonizados*, but *Daddy
Likee?* was the newest painting in this collection, painted in 2018.
   I asked Kukuli if she had done anything differently in this last
painting. She remarked that when she titled it *Daddy Likee?*, she
was for "the first time directly talking to that observer that has been

always judging my body." "When I exhibit in Peru," she explained, "questions always go into the sexual arena, instead of other things that were louder in the painting, like colonization, for instance, or for example, when women try to paint themselves, or try to look different so that they are whiter, trying to be the other in order to survive, or to think better of their own. In *Daddy Likee?* I feel I have much more awareness of how little I care."[114] She resists seeing nakedness as sexualization:

> There was never an intention of sexualizing my body; my body was sexualized by the eye of the beholder. So I would always say, no, there is no sexualization of my body, and they were really surprised, because . . . "no, but your body is naked." . . . So I was like, why does that necessarily imply a provocation or a flirtation with the audience? I am not standing in a particularly provoking way unless I am trying to give a message, like when I was pregnant, and I had my huge belly, and I was posing like Miss Universe because I think that I never saw myself as beautiful. But, in general, I never had the intention to shock because of the presence of my body.[115]

When Kukuli gave a talk at the Pennsylvania Academy of Fine Arts (PAFA), she mentioned that her father also pointed out the nakedness, but the painting's interpellation goes against the "familiar" in more than one sense. In response to expectations about beauty, Kukuli remarks, both ironically and seriously, that when she "achieved" menopause she felt liberated because she reached the status of nonobject: "I could say that I finally became a human being, if I wanted to be outrageous. . . . I felt freedom." So here, we have a painting where the artist represents herself pictorially as part of an artistic object that resists objectification.

Concerned with the lack of artists who are Black, Indigenous, or people of color in its permanent collection, PAFA acquired many new works, among them *Daddy Likee?*, in March 2019. It seems that their curatorial efforts turned around to respond to the interpellation. When I saw the painting on exhibition in this space, it really spoke back to the viewer, surrounded by many portraits of rich, white patrons from colonial Philadelphia who commissioned the paintings for themselves and their families. The performance of power and the power of performance are not the same, but they are related. Nowhere is this more evident in the artistic realm than in the relationship between beauty and violence.

Plunder Me Baby and Violence against Indigenous Women

While Kukuli's paintings seem to take the strategy of deconstruction, sculptures in *Plunder Me Baby* are more explicit about the relentless violence employed to marginalize women of color. The aesthetics of these ceramic pieces are informed by pre-Columbian art. In Cusco, where Kukuli grew up, it is almost impossible to avoid being imprinted with this cultural heritage. Kukuli points out that walking in the city, you can find old Inca walls everywhere. Machu Picchu is close by. Museums are filled with pre-Columbian work, and Kukuli's parents, both journalists, transmitted a pride for Cusco's rich cultural heritage to her from an early age:

> You cannot help but feed your eyes and aesthetic understanding from what you see. Because you are at the end what you saw when you were growing up. So I didn't have the opportunity to see a Velazquez or a Picasso, or a modern work firsthand, but I did see firsthand pre-Columbian works several times. That and that my parents were Cuzquenian chauvinists, so they made sure we were aware of our origins, our ancestry, and the aesthetics in terms of music, in terms of architecture.[116]

And yet, the admiration for the Inca or the Aztec of yesterday can coexist with contempt for the Indian of today. "Incas yes, Indians no" is an expression coined by the Peruvian historian Cecilia Méndez to portray a central feature of the ideology of Peruvian Creole nationalism.[117] The ceramic pieces address the unequal treatment of people, especially women, of native descent in Peru, who experience violence, in this case from Kukuli's own community of origin, the Peruvian middle class—a middle class where in-house maids and nannies are common, unlike in the United States. She directly asserts this, "I am talking about a middle-class Peruvian reality."[118] By pointing the critique at her own community, Kukuli performs what Anzaldúa once called new tribalism: "I must forsake 'home'"—that is, comfort zones, both personal and cultural—"every day of my life to keep burgeoning into the tree of myself."[119] She dedicates the series to her nanny, Lorenza, and to another person, also from a rural area, who works in her family home and who was like a second mother to her. Reading the letter to Lorenza, we learn about the gesture of empathic disempowerment that informs the collection. In this artistic statement, Kukuli describes the way that indigenous people are devalued through an anecdote featuring her sixteen-year-old nanny, Lorenza. The collection is a way to distill and share that awareness: the pieces all have racial slurs as titles, but at the same time Kukuli has her face on each one, as she did not want people to think that she was insulting others. She explains: "These pieces are awoke and are conscious of being observed. Each one of them is titled with a pejorative name, the same names that you and many of you and I have endured as a result of our indigenous ancestry."[120] The statement continues: "All these pieces have my face because I wanted to become each one of them to repossess properly my identity and to take each one of those pejorative epithets with combativeness."[121] As in her newest performance piece, the tactics consist of making a familiar face the target of violence.

The gesture echoes an empathic movement, putting her self in the faces of those who are denigrated. It also fights back by despising the colonial enterprise's ignorance and the ignorance of the artistic collections that entrap the high pre-Columbian art of her ancestors as ethnic objects dispossessed of aesthetic value. Making an art object that looks back at the colonial gaze elicits a change in the aesthetic Oxford use of empathy. The rejection camouflaged in the denounced cultural values cannot be projected *into* the piece because the piece talks back, spitting them out *onto* the viewer. The new tribalism that Anzaldúa speaks of poses a radical relationality that disassembles the network of behaviors oppressing the indigenous roots of Latin American identity. Yet "roots are embedded not only in the soil but also in inner city asphalt and in the spirit, psyche, incorporeal ground of being. . . . [W]e are also las cosas y la gente que pasan a nuestros alrededores [the things and people that happen all around us]."¹²²

It is pertinent, in closing, to revisit historian Paul Gilroy's invitation to not allocate histories of suffering exclusively to their victims. For Gilroy, "[t]his proposed change of perspective about the value of suffering is not then exclusively of interest to its victims and any kin who remember them. Because it is a matter of justice, it is not just an issue for the wronged "minorities" whose own lost or fading identities may be restored or rescued by the practice of commemoration."¹²³ Changing the perspective to go beyond binary options in empathy means to step out of the dichotomy victim-perpetrator, inhabiting the gray areas. For Dominick LaCapra, from an intellectual history point of view, "the deconstruction of binary opposites makes more not less demanding the problem of rearticulation and articulatory practices (including institutions)."¹²⁴ In *Touching Feeling*, Sedgwick takes on the performative potential of the gray areas in between binary opposites and critically condemns its exclusion, "[a]nother problem with reifying the status quo is what it does to the middle ranges of agency. One's relation to *what is* risks becoming reactive and bifurcated, that of a consumer: one's choices narrow to accepting or refusing (buying, not buying) this or that manifestation of it, dramatizing only the extremes of compulsion and voluntarity. Yet it is only the middle ranges of agency that offer space for effectual creativity and change."¹²⁵ The change of perspective proposed by Gilroy,

is also of concern to those who may have benefited directly and indirectly from the rational application of irrationality and barbarity. Perhaps, above all, this attempt to reconceptualize modernity so that it encompasses these possibilities is relevant to the majority who are unlikely to count themselves as affiliated with either of the principal groups: victims and perpetrators. This difficult stance challenges that unnamed group to witness suffering that pass beyond the reach of words and, in doing so, to see how an understanding of one's own particularity or identity might be transformed as a result of a principled exposure to the claims of otherness.[126]

In a sense, looking back at the colonial gaze demands a look at its treasured modernity.

We can now say that empathic thought that reaches out to imagine the conditions and contexts of other people must also take into consideration how that imagination has been coached by colonialism. It is necessary, then, to reach out beyond others as objects of analysis to acknowledge the others as subjects producing thought and analyses of their conditions. Empathic disempowerment as a practice of ethnographic refusal begins by acknowledging interpellations coming from the affected parties, but it gains strength when it can pose a radical relationality that "imagines alternatives to oppressive cultural norms."[127] A radical take on relationality consists in challenging the grid of intelligibility under which the other is known. This also refers to a form of seeking relations and social transformation outside the terms set by the current system, conceiving one's being as constituted through other beings.[128] In brief, the conditions and contexts we imagine have to imagine that other imaginations exist and are important.

A radical relationality creates avenues for relations that decentralize the powerful as interlocutor and position other "others" instead. In this way, it creates that which it cannot imagine, forming networks of different othered subject positions that can learn from each other by decolonizing colonial entropy. This allows us to rethink empathy's self-conscious attempts to imagine the conditions of other persons. Empathic disempowerment as anticolonial entropy entails questioning the technologies of liberty that maintain the status quo. Jaskiran Dhillon defines anticolonial entropy as "a network of ideas, beliefs and organizing efforts crucial to fostering a political condition of decolonial disorder in our current reality of racial capitalism, violent state sovereignty, and a persistent avowal of present and future where white settler power reigns supreme."[129]

This last chapter took up forms of empathic disempowerment that respond to or reiterate Gloria Anzaldúa's interpellation from the epigraph. The reiteration corresponds to a more contemporary interpellation conveyed by the Peruvian artist Kukuli Velarde. In addition to analyzing her work displayed at Taller Puertorriqueño's gallery in Philadelphia on the occasion of her solo exhibit *The Complicit Eye* and some of her other work, I evaluated the apology to the Lakota people delivered by Veterans Stand with Standing Rock at the protests against the Dakota Access Pipeline. Here, I considered the violence accompanying contact zones. This is in tune with a reading of empathic disempowerment as a form of liberation that advances anticolonial entropy by means of a radical take on relationality. Opening the field of forces to structural change is what anticolonial entropy is after. For this, the technologies of the self that maintain the status quo need to be constantly considered. For Dhillon, anticolonial entropy could be observed in the struggle against the Dakota Access Pipeline, but her notion could be also applied to interpret what we observe in a particular area that responds to tradition and its history within the arts.

Conclusion

THIS BOOK HAS PROPELLED a notion of empathy that can be succinctly summarized using activist Judy Vaughn's words, "You don't think your way into a different way of acting; you act your way into a different way of thinking."[1] This is just what the performers analyzed in each of the chapters have done. I considered emotions in relation to the role that the subject matter and the subject position play because their performances were read as enactments of power. In these enactments of power the act of performing identity offers diverse paths to intervene on the prevalent forms of interaction. Here a Latina dominates in *Indigurrito*, a Black Dominican-York disidentifies in *Dominicanish*, Cuban actors engage with dissimilar tales of displacement and disengagement, a white subject apologizes, and, in the end, a Peruvian woman flips the gaze to challenge it inward and outward. All of them engage in self-valuation and self-identification with different tools and strategies. The purpose of the different analyses accompanying each performance was never measuring empathy, but dealing with empathic thought.

We have begun and ended with a white man kneeling in a loop of enactments of power that mirror each other, and two women artists' response to the imposition of celebrating colonization. Perhaps the differential Ngũgĩ wa Thiong'o posed between the power of performance in the arts and the performance of power by the state is most apparent in the apology.[2] Yet, a study of heterotopias would demand that each and every staged body evaluates its relationship to a body of knowledge and its forms of life, as we create an environment in which affirmative statements are more than a target for moral deconstruction. Performance as a medium proposes to put the body in the space of representation and cope with it. The body, for a 'theory in the flesh,' "is the *expression* of evolving political consciousness, and the *creator* of consciousness itself."[3] Given the highly violent state of interactions currently prevailing in the US, we need to foster dialogues that train the mind in new forms of dualities. Dualities are graspable, so rather than discussing whether they should exist or not—because they, in fact, do exist—it can better serve empathy to supplement initial dualities with new dualities, as if they were lines of escape that create other exteriorities.[4] Multiplicities are better, but supplemental dualities seem to me a better way of reaching out to other forms of feeling.

I wanted this book's subtitle to be "This bridge called our America." Initially, I thought of this "bridge" as an exploration of connections in the establishment of subjective positions around the political. I lost the subtitle's battle, but the epigraph still stands. Over the process of writing this book, I also began to have in mind the burdens this exploration of connections transfers to minoritarian subjects and the areas of understanding it can obliterate, all crucial to an analysis of empathy. This type of exploration can be both empowering and draining.[5] In a piece from 1980 included in the foreword to the first edition of *This Bridge Called My Back*, Moraga asked: "How can we—this time—not use our bodies to be thrown over a river of tormented history to bridge the gap?"[6] And then she replied, "I cannot continue to use my body to be walked over to make a connection."[7] These words still resonate with our current reality in the United States. The fact that ethnic bodies are sometimes sought after not even to make connections, but to make simulacrums, broadens the significance of a focus on empathy in enactments of power. Anzaldúa and Cherríe Moraga's anthology was an act-of-healing project. The possibility of empathy in the performances presented in *Empathy and Performance* works in the same manner.

There is a "history of conquest" that not only "layered another country over a preexisting nation" but also put in motion a game of in-group/out-group divisions designed purely as enactments of power.[8] For Spillers, "America juxtaposes two referential systems:" "America" was "as much 'discovery' on the retinal surface as it was appropriation of land and historical subjects."[9] In Latinx America we came to know a pool of ways of life that circle around conquest, oppression, displacement, external and internal treats, internal and external apathy, collective strength, collective shame, and more. This work comes out in a time in which mass shootings targeting non-whites, non-straights, non-[identity] have become a constant in the United States; it would be naive to think of empathy as a magic potion to solve these crises, but it is not irrational to think that empathic thought nourishes the cultural ground where a healthy civic society grows. These performances introduced us to ways of readdressing the power of empathy to understand a staged body that is not the self. This is a body that contrarily to compassion, which creates a distance, is in the same stage. Elaborative empathy creates a space other for coexistent bodies in relation. This relation goes beyond looking at each other's social tags. The inhibition of empathy through identity categorizations can be better understood if one differentiates between spontaneous and elaborative empathy. Identity categories have great weight in the expression of subjectivities; this expression nonetheless, is not always afforded the necessary level of flexibility. The avenues opened for empowerment favor some paths and not others. During interactions that intervene on expectations, perception, and relationality, spontaneous empathy may be challenged when it produces a reading of power not in tune with a lived experience. By attending to procedures of cultural inheritance in Latinx America today and analyzing the difference between empathy's triggered and elaborated responses, we might be in a better place to perceive that readings of enactments of power are always part of a situated enactment of power, where we stand.

It is crucial to acknowledge that identity categorizations influence attention and care. *Indigurrito* showed how a performance opens the doors for empowerment to be conceptualized in more than one way. Like technology, identity categories are not bad per se; they can be used for good or ill. The performances analyzed in these pages show that artists can embrace, reject, distract, complicate, inform—and much more, by means of how they devise identity categories imaginatively to foster empathy. Perplexity can be crucial to evaluate which externally defined images we come up with when we get closer to other spaces for the self. I think this is what José Lezama Lima meant when he said that only what is difficult is stimulating.[10] Participatory empathy, as we examined it through an analysis of *¡Bienvenidos Blancos! or Welcome White People!*, is a moment of fructiferous intercultural encounter. It is rarely utopic, but it is usually enlightening. Emotional experiences benefit from giving a multidimensional rendering to power and its enactments. In this highly clustered society, capitalism and whiteness need to be reexamined. Empathy gains strength when it can generate a radical relationality that rehearses alternatives to oppressive cultural norms.

The concepts guiding each chapter—flesh, disidentification, the commons of the brown, and anticolonial entropy—were meant to resonate in the chapters that followed. The approach I took allowed me to begin with simple and straightforward skills and move toward more complex and subtle ones. Performance is an ideal medium to see how identity categorizations influence openness to understanding emotional experiences. Hence, questions about how we understand and reconfigure intersubjective experience seem especially fit. Parallel and complementary emotions inform empathy's limits and nuances. If empathy is the space of concern for others, the notion of limits affects the transformational prospects of its private and public space. Once there is an openness to perceive different identity categories, some of which might not always be obvious, this perception can be further explored. Taken as "a mechanism that bridges the gap between experience and thought," empathy reveals how crucial is to avoid conflating identities with emotional experiences.[11]

In order for a bridge to be needed, a gap needs to be perceived, to motivate and sustain the effort that goes into elaborative empathy. This is particularly relevant when considering how emotional episodes serve as models in the links we establish between emotional memories and empathy.[12] The psychic borderlands and the violence accompanying the colonization of the Americas serve as the material reality for Moraga's "theory in the flesh." Spillers's theoretical framework allows us to take flesh as the point of entrance to a culture that shows the scars it inflicts on modern psyches; that is, "flesh" as a cultural text whose inside has been turned outside.[13] Flesh is the "zero degree of social conceptualization" only because it is unmarked, not *realized*.[14] Puzzlement has a vital role in the link between emotional memories and empathy in the cases in which modeling falls short. Puzzlement makes us curious about what we do not know. As a toolbox, empathy (a) sustains civil society and human dignity through an ability to imagine new intersubjective consciousness, (b) gives others the benefit of perceptual doubt, and (c) creates intersubjective imaginaries.[15] These abilities were actively explored in the selected scenes of interaction. Encoding—that is, how we read emotional expressions and situations—is informed by an array of elements. Anticolonial entropy, a concept introduced in the last chapter, allowed us to consider disempowerment of pride based on domination as an alternative to open new gaps in the psychic borderlands where empathy can thrive. *Corporealizations* can take many avenues, and I have attempted to explore a variety of them through the different analyses of these performances and their creative efforts to intervene on interactions.

I included these performances as a way of thinking today, within the realm of contemporary problems, about the dramatized dilemma of cultural understanding (and misunderstanding) and the exploration of subaltern identities. An express takeaway summary would read like this: identity categories influence our openness to understanding (at least we should know this); disidentification maintains a tension that can open reflection on emotional memories (maybe one day we can use this); feeling entails subject positions (this comes in handy in intercultural exchanges); and empathic disempowerment can help *corporealize* psychic borderlands (small doses recommended, a vaccine for the lobbying powerful would be splendid). If the agenda of *Empathy and Performance* needed to be summarized in a sentence, it would be this: it wants you to go beyond spontaneous empathy, to prepare yourself to be puzzled, to participate, and to see the other as a producer of readings of reality and theories of the self.

NOTES

INTRODUCTION

1. By then (1891), the notion of *nuestra América* had been in circulation for a while. I believe this essay followed in the steps of works by the Colombian journalist and politician José María Torres Caicedo (such as "Las dos Américas" and "Union Latino-Americana" from 1857 and 1865) and the Chilean intellectual Francisco Bilbao ("La definición," "La América en peligro," and "Iniciativa de la América" from 1851 and 1856).

2. Altamirano, *La invención de Nuestra América*, 41–42. Carlos Altamirano notes that in the nineteenth century and in the American republics, the projects tending to a transcontinental Hispanic union followed, in the first stage, the objective of defending the independence of these nations from Spain's aims at reconquering them and in general, from the imperial ambitions of Europe. When the Spanish-speaking American nations began to perceive the threat of the United States' expansionist drive, the notion of *our America* began to circulate, dividing the American continent in two counterposed worlds: one with its predominant pragmatism and individualism; the other characterized by its spiritualism and sociability. Altamirano, *La invención*, 41–42, 63–65, 78–79.

3. Laura E. Gómez presents in *Inventing Latinos* an excellent study of how and why the Latinx identity is becoming a distinctive racial identity in the US.

4. Kinship positions entail membership in a group identity, which can be willing or unwilling. Two networks of feeling and support, or lack thereof, are at play here.

5. Fusco, *English Is Broken Here*, see specifically "The Other History of Intercultural Performance," 37–63, 38.

6. Lewis, "Abroad at Home," 17. See also Zelizer, "30 Issues."

7. Sherry, "Home Fires," 75.

8. Fusco, *English is Broken Here*, 38.

9. Pérez Firmat, *Life on the Hyphen: The Cuban-American Way.*

10. Blankenbuehler, "Cashing in on Standing Rock."

11. Associated Press, "A Man Pleads Guilty to Federal Charges in the El Paso Shooting that Targeted Latinos."

12. Schneider, *The Explicit Body in Performance*, 178.

13. I am mainly referring to the US here, but I employ the term to keep in mind that historically, "American" refers to a long established identitarian narrative of self-representation, beginning in the nineteenth century. See Altamirano, *La invención de Nuestra América*.

14. Hogan, *What Literature Teaches Us*, 73–75.

15. Hogan, *What Literature Teaches Us*, 73–75.

16. Hogan, *What Literature Teaches Us*, 75.

17. For the notion of "form of life," see Wittgenstein, *Philosophical Investigations*, par. 241.

18. Ngũgĩ wa Thiong'o, "Enactments of Power," 11–30.

19. Hammond, *Empathy and the Psychology of Literary Modernism*, 6–7.

20. Plamper, *The History of Emotions*, 248.

21. Plamper, *The History of Emotions*, 248–49.

22. Hogan, *What Literature Teaches Us*, 75.

23. Hogan, *What Literature Teaches Us*, 58.

24. Hogan, *What Literature Teaches Us*, 58.

25. Wilkerson, *Caste*, 69.

26. She then places this critique of seeing awareness as change in the context of scholarship, "To a startling extent, the articulations of New Historicist scholarship rely on the prestige of a single, overarching narrative: exposing and problematizing hidden violences in the genealogy of the modern liberal subject." Sedgwick, *Touching Feeling*, 139.

27. Phelan, "Performance, Live Culture and Things of the Heart," 293–94.

28. Hogan, *What Literature Teaches Us*, 68.

29. Hogan, *What Literature Teaches Us*, 68.

30. Maibom, *Empathy and Morality*, 21

31. Sawin, *Performance at the Nexus of Gender, Power, and Desire*, 41.

32. Fusco, *English Is Broken Here*, 40.

33. Muñoz, "Feeling Brown," 69.

34. Spillers, *Black, White, and in Color*, 131.

35. Scheer, "Topographies of Emotion," 34–35.

36. Lanzoni, *Empathy: A History*, ix, 2.

37. Maibom, *Empathy and Morality*, 2n1; Calloway-Thomas, *Empathy in the Global World*, 6.

38. Hammond, *Empathy and the Psychology of Literary Modernism*, 179.

39. Maibom, *Empathy and Morality*, 10.

40. Maibom, *Empathy and Morality*, 9.

41. Maibom, *Empathy and Morality*, 13.

42. Maibom, *Empathy and Morality*, 2.

43. R. Hogan, "Development of an Empathy Scale," 307–16.

44. Bryant, "An Index of Empathy for Children and Adolescents," 413–25.

45. Maibom, *Empathy and Morality*, 20.

46. Jolliffe and Farrington, "Development and Validation of the Basic Empathy Scale," 589–611.

47. Jolliffe and Farrington, "Development and Validation," 601.

48. Bloom, *Against Empathy*, 121.

49. Maibom, *Empathy and Morality*, 21.
50. Maibom, *Empathy and Morality*, 19.
51. Maibom, *Empathy and Morality*, 20.
52. Lanzoni, *Empathy*, 217.
53. Gonnerman, "The Interview," 44.
54. Lanzoni, *Empathy*, 249.
55. Hogan, *What Literature*, 70. For work on emotional standards, see Stearns, "Emotionology: Clarifying the History," and Reddy, "Historical Research on the Self and Emotions."
56. Lanzoni, *Empathy*, 6.
57. Lanzoni, *Empathy*, 238.
58. Spillers, *Black, White, and in Color*, 205.
59. Lanzoni, *Empathy*, 246.
60. Maibom, *Empathy and Morality*, 236.
61. Spillers, *Black, White, and in Color*, 206–7.
62. Moraga, *This Bridge Called My Back*, 19.
63. Hogan, *What Literature Teaches Us*, 75.
64. Hammond, *Empathy and the Psychology of Literary Modernism*, 177.
65. Anzaldúa, *Borderlands*, 107–8.

CHAPTER 1

Acknowledgment: This chapter is derived in part from an article, "Empathy and Flesh in Performance," published in *Journal of Latinos and Education* (2022) copyright Taylor & Francis, available online: https://www.tandfonline.com/doi/10.1080/15348431.2022.2107519.

1. Lanzoni, *Empathy*, x.
2. Lanzoni, *Empathy*, 5–6.
3. Lanzoni, *Empathy*, 6.
4. Rivera, "Alex Rivera Speaking at Platform Summit 2014." YouTube, November 19, video, 18:13. www.youtube.com/watch?v=eHPsmfLdiUs.
5. Spillers, *Black, White, and in Color*, 332.
6. Spillers, *Black, White, and in Color*, 204–206.
7. Spillers, *Black, White, and in Color*, 206.
8. Wilkerson, *Caste*, 49.
9. Spillers, *Black, White, and in Color*, 206.
10. Moraga, *This Bridge Called My Back*, 23.
11. Moraga, *This Bridge Called My Back*, 23.
12. Lima, *The Latino Body*, 169–70.
13. Spillers, *Black, White, and in Color*, 327.
14. McGarry, "The New Muse | Nao Bustamante."
15. Foucault, "Des espaces autres (conférence au Cercle d'études architecturales, 14 mars 1967)," 46–49. According to Etienne Balibar, Foucault initially thought of these as spaces of transgression that could model possible alternative spaces, but later rejected this. Balibar, "Utopia 1/13."

16. Interview by the author with author and performer Nao Bustamante, December 20, 2019. Hereinafter cited as Bustamante interview.

17. "*Indigurrito* (1992)," Hemispheric Institute of Performance, https://hemisphericinstitute.org/en/hidvl-collections/item/1290-nao-indigurrito.html.

18. Martínez, *On Making Sense*, 80–81.

19. Febvre, *A New Kind of History*, 215.

20. Bustamante interview.

21. Good Vibrations, based in San Francisco since 1977, was one of the first female-oriented sex-shops in the country. As Paul B. Preciado states, it was "feminine y feminist"; the company, founded by Joani Blank, was the first one exclusively dedicated to female and lesbian pleasure. Preciado, *Manifesto contrasexual*, 109n54, 256.

22. Bustamante interview.

23. Alvarado, *Abject Performances*, 111.

24. Alvarado, *Abject Performances*, 111.

25. Muñoz quoted in Alvarado, *Abject Performances*, 118.

26. Alvarado, *Abject Performances*, 118.

27. Spillers, *Black, White, and in Color*, 220, 280–81.

28. Spillers, *Black, White, and in Color*, 280–81.

29. Spillers, *Black, White, and in Color*, 206.

30. Gordon quoted in Alvarado, "Ghostly Givings," 246.

31. Bustamante interview, my emphasis.

32. Burt, "'She's Leaving Home,'" 66.

33. Hogan, *What Literature Teaches Us*, 75.

34. Bustamante interview.

35. Bustamante interview.

36. Ngũgĩ, "Enactments of Power," 13.

37. Ngũgĩ, "Enactments of Power," 12–13.

38. At this time his play *I Will Marry When I Want / Ngaahika Ndeenda* was produced and staged, but it was banned after six weeks for "alleged portrayal of post-colonial struggles that harmed citizens." It was banned again in 1990 and finally, after thirty-two years, put on stage at the Kenya National Theatre from May 22 to May 29, 2022. It features prominent themes on hypocrisy, corruption of religion, capitalism, and politics. It is believed that the play was the cause of Ngũgĩ wa Thiong'o's arrest in 1977. One year later, after the death of Mzee Jomo Kenyatta, he was released and went into exile. See Kenya News, "Ngugi wa Thiong'o play back after 32 years."

39. Ngũgĩ wa Thiong'o, "Enactments of Power," 11.

40. Smith quotes in Spillers, *Black, White, and in Color*, 335.

41. Spillers, *Black, White, and in Color*, 324, 327.

42. Spillers, *Black, White, and in Color*, 327.

43. Foucault defines *dispositif* as a heterogeneous network linking discourses, institutions, laws, and the like. It is what articulates power and knowledge; it might change relationality while still assuring the continuation of a structure of relations. Foucault, *Power/Knowledge*, 194.

44. Bustamante interview.

45. Bustamante interview.
46. Currie, "Empathy for Objects"; Smith cited in Matravers, *Empathy*, 131.
47. Bustamante interview.
48. Matravers, *Empathy*, 124–27.
49. Matravers, *Empathy*, 135
50. Matravers, *Empathy*, 135.
51. LaCapra, *Understanding Others*, 47, 146.
52. LaCapra, *Understanding Others*, 48.
53. Spillers, *Black, White, and in Color*, 280–81.
54. Martínez, *On Making Sense*, 81.
55. Bustamante interview.
56. Hammond, *Empathy and the Psychology of Literary Modernism*, 4.
57. Spillers, *Black, White, and in Color*, 131.
58. Spillers, *Black, White, and in Color*, 131.
59. Bustamante, *Indigurrito.*
60. Bustamante interview.
61. Felski, *Beyond Feminist*, 7.
62. Schneider, *The Explicit Body in Performance*, 65.
63. Phelan, "Performance, Live Culture and Things of the Heart," 295.
64. See DuBois, *The Souls;* Gilroy, *The Black Atlantic.*
65. Spillers, *Black, White, and in Color*, 206.
66. Hogan, *What Literature Teaches Us*, 57.
67. Hogan, *What Literature Teaches Us*, 65–68.
68. After interviewing Nao Bustamante, I learned that the person was a dancer acting "goofy." Bustamante did not prompt him to do so.
69. Bustamante interview.
70. Sawin, "Performance at the Nexus," 44.
71. Sawin, "Performance at the Nexus," 45.
72. Bustamante interview.
73. Spillers, *Black, White, and in Color*, 204.
74. Wilkerson, *Caste*, 124

CHAPTER 2

Epigraph. Báez, "Lectura y coloquio," 1:02:00.
1. Casamayor-Cisneros, "Confrontation and Occurrence," 130.
2. Casamayor-Cisneros, "Confrontation and Occurrence," 121.
3. Collins, "Learning from the Outsider Within,"16–17.
4. Collins, "Learning from the Outsider Within," 16, 18.
5. García Peña, "Performing Identity, Language, and Resistance," 40.
6. Stevens, *Aquí y Allá*, 154.
7. García Peña, *Translating Blackness*, 14.
8. De La Fuente, "Los afrolatinos y los estudios afrolatinoamericanos," 207.
9. García Peña, *Translating Blackness*, 4.
10. García Peña, *Translating Blackness*, 20. In "Bodies and Memories: Afrolatina Identities in Motion," Ana Maurine Lara showed the pros and cons

of this coming and going. She began this essay with an anecdote about how after thinking that she was returning to the DR for good, she had to leave after nine months, "mostly because I couldn't get a job," "That piece had everything to do with my perceived race and class. At the time, I had dreadlocks" (41). Yet, when she encounters a Dominican that doesn't have a US citizenship like her, who has to straighten her hair to get a job, she concludes that "So it was ironic that I, dreadlocks and all US privilege, was sitting with someone who had to straighten her hair in order to get employment, in a place where I was being ignored because of my presentation. I could afford to be indignant because I could leave to get a job elsewhere" (43–44).

11. Propst, "Josefina Baez' *Dominicanish* Part of Harlem Stage's Fall Season."
12. Interview by the author with author and performer Josefina Báez, June 22, 2020. Hereinafter cited as Báez interview. It is usually danced for Lent; a recording of it from 2011 is available here: "GAGÁ de la Ceja. La Romana, República Dominicana," YouTube, posted by Pels Saúco, May 17, 2011, www.youtube.com/watch?v=owJbpImu-Ns.
13. They would also puzzle people familiar with the traditional Kuchipudi form because they are mixed with theater biomechanics. Durán Almarza, "At Home at the Border," 59.
14. A reviewer once questioned the distinction between having an accent and not having an accent. At a theoretical level we all know that even "unaccented" English always has an accent; at the practical level, for a person with an accent, the difference in the actual relationship with the language experience requires no explanation. To have an accent means to be marked, instantly labeled with identity categorizations, infused in questions, exoticization, use or distrust, fear, or interest; being marked means to be pressed into a variety of types of "other" that the nonlocal pronunciation and enunciation could point to. For more on this topic, see *English with an Accent* by R. Barrett, J. Cramer, and K. McGowan.
15. Stevens, *Aquí y Allá*, 151–52.
16. Stevens, *Aquí y Allá*, 147.
17. Joaquín Balaguer was vice president of the Dominican Republic from 1957 to 1960, and president from 1960–1962, 1966–1978, and 1986–1996. He is widely considered one crucial developer of the anti-Haitian ideology that began to forcefully be established during the Trujillo years. In the 1994 elections, when Balaguer run against José Francisco Peña, part of the strategy of his campaign was to stir fear about Peña's Haitian ancestry. In 2000, at ninety-four years old and completely blind, he ran for a seventh presidential term, but was defeated.
18. "Many Haitians Leave Dominican Republic after Court Decision," *Morning Edition*, NPR, Nov. 28, 2013, https://www.npr.org/2013/11/28/247635908/many-haitians-leave-dominican-republic-after-court-decision
19. Durán Almarza, "At Home at the Border," 55.
20. García Peña, "Performing," 34.

21. The Trujillo regime preferred the term *indio* primarily because it was devoid of any semantic allusion to an African heritage. Torres-Saillant, "The Tribulations of Blackness," 139.
22. Báez interview.
23. Torres-Saillant, *Desde la orilla*, cited in Josefina Báez website.
24. Torres-Saillant, "The Tribulations of Blackness," 129.
25. sarahfuller12345, "Adrian Piper 'Cornered.'" *GCOP200* (blog), February 6, 2014. sarahfullergcop200.wordpress.com/2014/02/06/adrian-piper-cornered.
26. Costello and Vickery, *Art: Key Contemporary Thinkers*, 42.
27. Collins "Learning from the Outsider Within," 32.
28. Collins "Learning from the Outsider Within," 24.
29. bell hooks, cited in Collins, "Learning from the Outsider Within," 20.
30. Báez interview.
31. Maillo-Pozo, "Home Is Where," 68.
32. Stevens, *Aquí y Allá*, 154.
33. García Peña 2018, 173, cited in Stevens, *Aquí y Allá*, 154.
34. Báez, *Dominicanish*, with photographs by Giovanni Savino, 45.
35. Nowadays, she only does one-on-one retreats; this new format began even before the COVID-19 pandemic.
36. Báez "Lectura y coloquio."
37. Báez "Lectura y coloquio."
38. Báez, *Latin in: antología de autología*, 3.
39. Guillén, "Yo, Oy Yo," 6.
40. Báez interview.
41. Cep, "Rescue Work," 28.
42. Báez interview.
43. García Peña, *Translating Blackness*, 2.
44. Báez interview.
45. Hogan, *What Literature*, 66.
46. Algarín, *Survival*, 15.
47. Báez interview.
48. Durán Almarza, "At Home at the Border," 53. In an essay published earlier, García Peña came to a similar conclusion, although from a point of view focused on Dominican national identity discourse: "[T]he notion of Negro or noir, which was equated to Haitian, had to be erased from the discourse of the emerging Dominican state. As a result, the Dominican Republic in its formation was conceived as a hybrid nation where there could only be one race: the newly created Dominican race. This construction privileged Hispanic language, history, and culture and claimed the long-lost Taíno indigenous heritage. In this context, to claim one's Dominican and black identities represents a contradiction, as well as a challenge of Dominican national identity." García Peña, "Performing Identity," 33.
49. García Peña, "Performing Identity," 30.

50. Szalita, "Some Thoughts on Empathy," 108.
51. García Peña, "Performing Identity," 33.
52. García Peña, "Performing Identity," 34.
53. Báez interview.
54. Cavanaugh, *The Spark*, 135.
55. Cavanaugh, *The Spark*, 135.
56. Cavanaugh, *The Spark*, 124.
57. Cited in Cavanaugh, *The Spark*, 124.
58. Jill Lepore in "Data-driven," points to another problem arising in the horizon with the corporative preference for privileging a data science approach that excludes any other approach, "A problem for humanity though, is that lately people seem to want to tug open only the bottom drawer, 'Data,' as if it were the only place you can find any answers, as if only data tells because only data sells" (17).
59. Cavanaugh, *The Spark*, 53.
60. Hogan, *What Literature*, 67.
61. Hogan, *What Literature*, 56.
62. Hogan, *What Literature*, 56.
63. Lisa Jevis's blog entry for PM Press "The End of Feminism's Third Wave" (https://blog.pmpress.org/2019/08/13/the-end-of-feminisms-third-wave) provides a great example of what this looks like and what is at stake. It was originally published in *Ms Magazine*.
64. Báez interview.
65. Báez interview.
66. Matravers, *Empathy*, 103.
67. Hogan, *What Literature*, 65.
68. Especially nowadays, when we are observing that following a marketing and philanthropy push in university contexts and corporations at large, PR policy prioritizes aggressively virtue signaling strategies, which supplement the current monetization of "diversity" at the service of data brokers and AI model training.
69. Hogan, *Affective Narratology*, 5.
70. Hogan, *What Literature*, 58.
71. Lanzoni, *Empathy: A History*, x.
72. Lanzoni, *Empathy: A History*, x.
73. Szalita, "Some Thoughts on Empathy," 110.
74. Muñoz, *Disidentifications*, 25.
75. Muñoz, *Disidentifications*, 179.
76. Althusser's interpellation claims that skills and cultural values are reproduced by the ideological state apparatuses: the school, the church, the health system, and so forth, thus forming subjects. He sought to add to a Marxist view of the superstructure, focusing on how cultural values are reproduced as to be taken for granted.
77. Muñoz, *Disidentifications*, 28.
78. Muñoz, *Disidentifications*, 55.
79. Pêcheux, *Language, Semantics and Ideology*, 158.

80. Báez interview.

81. Pêcheux, *Language, Semantics and Ideology*, 158.

82. Pêcheux, *Language, Semantics and Ideology*, 159.

83. Pêcheux, *Language, Semantics and Ideology*, 159.

84. Muñoz, *Disidentifications*, 31. Muñoz was here in tune with what Balibar's "Utopia 1/13" refers to as Foucault's early understanding of heterotopias as spaces of transgression that might teach us how to construct alternative models to the utopian/dystopian model of thinking.

85. García Peña, "Performing Identity," 32–33.

86. Báez interview.

87. Báez interview.

88. Muñoz, *Disidentifications*, 161.

89. Muñoz, *Disidentifications*, 179. Counterpublics are spheres that stand in opposition to the racism and homophobia of the dominant public sphere, and communities and relational chains of resistance that contest the dominant public sphere. The notion derives from Nancy Fraser's reworking of the Habermasian public sphere to allow for a contestation of the bourgeois public sphere, "elaborating alternative styles of political behavior and alternative norms of public speech." Muñoz, *Disidentifications*, 143, 146–147.

90. A particularly lucid analysis of this phenomenon might be exemplified by Olúfẹ́mi Táíwò 's *Elite Capture* or his article with Enzo Rossi): "What's New about Woke Racial Capitalism (and What Isn't): 'Wokewashing' and the Limits of Representation," that can be downloaded here: https://philpapers.org/rec/ROSWNA-2. Sean Illing interviewed Táíwò in *The Gray Area* podcast episode "Elites Have Captured Identity Politics," https://www.listennotes.com/podcasts/the-gray-area-with/elites-have-captured-IYPSmGtNua_/.

91. Cited in Hogan, *What Literature*, 50.

92. Cited in Hogan, *What Literature*, 49–51.

93. Báez interview.

CHAPTER 3

Epigraph. Howard Shapiro, "¡*Bienvenidos Blancos!—Welcome White People!*— to Cuba, from Team Sunshine," *Shapiro on Theater* (blog), WHYY, April 23, 2018, https://whyy.org/articles/bienvenidos-blancos-welcome-white-people-to-cuba-from-team-sunshine.

1. At the time of his death, Muñoz was working on "The Sense of Brown," which was published at the end of 2020. A fragment of the preface was published in *GLQ* in 2018. Muñoz had presented parts of it in a dialogue with Samuel Delany in 2013.

2. Calloway-Thomas, *Empathy in the Global World*; Hammond, *Empathy and the Psychology of Literary Modernism*, 177.

3. Dukes et al., "The Rise of Affectivism," 816. This article on the rise of affectivism appeared in June 2021 in *Nature Human Behaviour.* The issue

of "what matters" posed in this article coming from the field of science resonates with Sedwick's concern for "what motivates," exhibiting a more flexible take on epistemology.

4. Calloway-Thomas, *Empathy in the Global World*, 13.

5. Sedgwick, *Touching Feeling*, 17.

6. "Bienvenidos Blancos! or Welcome White People!" Swarthmore College Theater, https://www.swarthmore.edu/cooper-series/bienvenidos-blancos-or-welcome-white-people

7. Interview by the author with director and lead artist Alex Torra, June 12, 2020. Emphasis my own. Hereafter cited as Torra interview.

8. Anzaldúa, "Foreword to the Second Edition, 1983," 253.

9. Algarín, *Survival*, 1.

10. Torra interview.

11. See Alan Aja for an extensive study of Cuban privilege in the US, or Capó Crucet's chapter "Going Cowboy" for an autofictional take on it.

12. Torra interview.

13. Hogan, *What Literature*, 69; Cavanaugh, *The Spark*, 53.

14. Calloway-Thomas, *Empathy in the Global World*, 4.

15. Calloway-Thomas, *Empathy in the Global World*, 4.

16. Calloway-Thomas, *Empathy in the Global World*, 5.

17. Calloway-Thomas, *Empathy in the Global World*, 12.

18. Calloway-Thomas, *Empathy in the Global World*, 11–12.

19. Torra interview.

20. Torra interview.

21. Torra interview.

22. Torra interview.

23. Torra interview.

24. Torra interview.

25. Calloway-Thomas, *Empathy in the Global World*, 13.

26. Gilroy, *Against Race*, 99.

27. Torra interview, my emphasis.

28. Gilroy, *Against Race*, 99.

29. Capó Crucet, *My Time among the Whites*, 63–64.

30. Capó Crucet, *My Time among the Whites*, 82.

31. Torra interview, my emphasis. Perhaps, Torra was not aware of the other type of fantasy marketed to Cuban-Americans, the one that informs a connection to an identity or identity-resolution time-shares.

32. Calloway-Thomas, *Empathy in the Global World*, 177–178.

33. Calloway-Thomas, *Empathy in the Global World*, 8. To do this, she advances a pedagogy of empathy. That is, "knowledge and information-based skills that help global citizens respond to and manage intercultural encounters caringly and competently" (214). In one more recent article, she suggests imagining a new "inter-subjective consciousness by undertaking the construction of templates of empathetic literacy that reach into classrooms, courtrooms, . . . and virtually via social media." "A Call for a Pedagogy of Empathy," 496.

34. Calloway-Thomas, "A Call for a Pedagogy of Empathy," 496.
35. Calloway-Thomas, "A Call for a Pedagogy of Empathy," 496.
36. Capó Crucet, *My Time Among the Whites*, 40.
37. Personal conversation by the author with the actress Jenna Horton, July 9, 2020.
38. See Delgado, "Spiritual Capital."
39. Delgado, "Spiritual Capital," 55–56.
40. "El régimen echa mano a otro decreto-ley para acallar las denuncias en tiempos de Covid-19." *Diario de Cuba*, April 22, 2020. diariodecuba.com/derechos-humanos/1587586651_17197.html; "Multado con 3.000 pesos un activista cubano por sus publicaciones en Facebook." *Diario de Cuba*, April 23, 2020. diariodecuba.com/derechos-humanos/1587655598_17316.html.
41. Landrove, *A un año del 11–J* (I). Rialta.org, June 21, 2022. https://rialta.org/podcast-aniversario-11j-i/. Hilda Landrove mentions among her sources the collective Justicia 11–J, a women activists group that has been working, among other tasks, to find the names of those in jail, since there is no public record available and independent journalism is scarce and relentlessly curtailed.
42. "Cuba Tightens Control of Internet after Protests." *BBC News*, August 18, 2021. https://www.bbc.com/news/world-latin-america-58255554
43. The new penal code even has a line criminalizing the use of constitutional rights, when it added that one "can not *arbitrarily* exercise a right or liberty recognized in the Cuban Constitution that puts at risk the Constitutional order and normal functioning of the Cuban State and Government." See Pidorych, junio 3, 2022. Glosas al nuevo Código Penal cubano in *El Estornudo*. https://revistaelestornudo.com/codigo-penal-cubano/
44. Bruguera, "Dignity has No Nationality."
45. Bruguera, "Dignity has No Nationality."
46. Fusco, Coco. *Dangerous moves*, 40.
47. Calloway-Thomas, *Empathy in the Global World*, 214.
48. Acts 1 and 4 did not significantly change.
49. Hogan, *What Literature*, 70.
50. Hogan, *What Literature*, 70.
51. Pêcheux, *Language, Semantics and Ideology*, 158.
52. Muñoz, *Disidentifications*, 179; Durán Almarza, "'At Home at the Border,'" 66.
53. Torra interview.
54. Torra interview.
55. Among them, "The Sense of Brown," which was published at the end of 2020.
56. Muñoz, José Esteban. "Fragment," 395.
57. Muñoz, José Esteban. "Fragment," 396.
58. Torra interview.
59. Rivers, "Apathy," 143 in *A New Handbook of Rhetoric*, 139–54. Michele Kennerly points to this emotional rerouting in the introduction; Rivers

pointed out that she suggested that it can be also analogous to an interruption of *groupfeeling*, where one mode of thinking blocks out alternate modes of thought. See 153n12.

60. "The History of Protests." www.npr.org/2020/06/01/867256404/the-history-of-protests-in-los-angeles-what-has-changed-since-the-rodney-king-ri.

61. Anzaldúa, *Light in the Dark*, 152.

62. Anzaldúa, *Light in the Dark*, 152.

63. Laura Lomas in "The Unbreakable Voice in a Minor Language" poses that Martí launched a history of Latino writing in New York characterized for maintaining uneasy relations to both the host country and the homeland's literature. For Lomas, what defines this literature is "an aesthetic and dialogic engagement with a minor language" (24). An emphasis on empathy allows for a more encompassing view on cultural production.

64. NPR, "The History of Protests."

65. The idea of a true Cuba, and who are true Cubans, encounters many nuances. One critical distinction lies in the relationship between people in exile and people on the island. In addition to the debate about people who were not born or raised on the island, which Alex Torra experiences, some argue that those who left after the 1959 revolution are not true Cubans, or lost their "Cubanness" through assimilation.

66. "Listen to Highlights from Acknowledgement." www.wrti.org/post/listen-highlights-acknowledgement-how-music-responds-wrti-901.

67. Rankine, *Just Us*, 251.

68. Rankine, *Just Us*, 245.

69. Colonial, authoritarian, and/ or discriminatory projects tend to leave open different proxy approaches to power. In the chapter "Arriving at Apostasy: Performing Testimonies of Ambivalent Belonging," Leticia Alvarado studied the link between expansionism and religion exploring the relation of Latino Mormons to Lamanite identity. Alvarado here shows "how an assertion of whiteness is embedded in the Latter Day Saints doctrine and lived practice that reveals the internalized racism that Latino members of the church navigate in an ambivalent belonging." *Abject Performances*, 140, 155.

70. Stevens, *Aquí y Allá*, 130.

71. Rankine, *Just Us*, 253.

72. Calloway-Thomas, "A Call for a Pedagogy of Empathy," 496–498.

73. "What Does White Allyship Look Like at This Moment? www.wnycstudios.org/podcasts/takeaway/segments/what-does-white-allyship-look-moment.

74. Torra interview, my emphasis.

CHAPTER 4

Epigraph. Anzaldúa, *Borderlands*, 107–8.

1. Anzaldúa, *Borderlands*, 107–8.

2. Fanon, *Black Skin, White Masks*.

3. Anzaldúa, *Borderlands*, 108.

4. "Wesley Clark Jr. Apologizes to the Lakota Nation." www.youtube.com/watch?v=FWU1NBcElSQ.

5. Since this event, the pipeline experienced massive spills. "In November 2017, Keystone 1, a sister project of Keystone XL, leaked more than 9,700 barrels of oil onto lands just west of the Sisseton Wahpeton Oyate's reservation in present-day South Dakota." "Uprising 12/13." Alleen Brown writing for *The Intercept* reported five spills in 2017. Brown, "Five Spills."

6. Van Gelder, "Why I Knelt."

7. Van Gelder, "Why I Knelt."

8. Interview by the author with publisher and editor of *Native News Online* Levi Rickert, December 22, 2022. Hereinafter cited as Rickert interview.

9. "Wesley Clark Jr. Apologizes to the Lakota Nation." www.youtube.com/watch?v=FWU1NBcElSQ.

10. Austin, *How to Do Things*, 83, cited in Ahmed, *The Cultural Politics of Emotion*, 114.

11. Ahmed, *The Cultural Politics of Emotion*, 115.

12. Rickert interview. Levi Rickert (Prairie Band Potawatomi Nation) is the editor and publisher of Tribal Business News, as well as the founder, publisher, and editor of Native News Online. *Tribal Business News* is a digital publication delivering in-depth stories, analysis, and business intelligence on all aspects of Native business and economic development activities. This platform is s a comprehensive 24/7 tool for tribes, tribal entities, policy makers, and anyone doing business in Indian Country. A lifelong resident of Grand Rapids, Michigan, Rickert is the former executive director of the North American Indian Center of Grand Rapids and currently sits on the Grand Valley State University Native American Advisory Board.

13. Van Gelder, "Why I Knelt."

14. According to Rickert, Crow Dog was part of the renewal of Native American culture. He worked very closely with the American Indian Movement: "Before . . . we could not celebrate who we were as Native Americans. . . . We have now the American Religious Freedom Act (1978). Jimmy Carter signed it into law. Crow Dog was part of that movement . . . and because of that I think it was pretty significant." Rickert interview.

15. Van Gelder, "Why I Knelt."

16. Clark was raised around the military and loved his upbringing. His father and namesake is retired U.S. Army general Wesley Clark Sr., formerly the supreme commander of NATO's military forces. He is a Georgetown-educated screenwriter and activist. Clark Jr. served four years in the Army and has become an active voice against the type of military action he observed when his friends enlisted after 9/11. Here is an interview that provides a good account of Clark's perspective and background, published on the same day he delivered the apology, on Dec. 5, 2016: https://www.salon.com/2016/12/05/wes-clark-jr-at-standing-rock-generals-activist-son-heads-to-n-d-driven-by-spiritual-fire-and-ready-to-be-killed/

17. Willis, former special assistant for Indian affairs in the US Department of Labor, and one of the panelists for "Uprising 12/13."

18. Dhillon, "Uprising 12/13," 1:34.
19. Rickert interview.
20. Van Gelder, "Why I Knelt."
21. Althusser, "Ideology and Ideological," 118.
22. Rickert interview.
23. Rickert interview.
24. Rickert interview.
25. Monet, "At Standing Rock, a Fight for Basic Survival." Monet holds an MA in international politics from Columbia Journalism School with a concentration in Indigenous human rights policy, and is Kawaik'a, a tribal citizen of Laguna Pueblo, Big Turkey clan—a Native nation in present-day New Mexico.
26. Manape LaMere is a Dakota/Ho- Chunk native and an appointee of the Oceti Sakowin Headsman Council, part of the multi-tiered camp leadership. Monet, "At Standing Rock, a Fight for Basic Survival."
27. Monet, "At Standing Rock, a Fight for Basic Survival." Monet reports that, "as contractors hired by the tribe began cleaning up the main camp, there had been no changes to the blockade. Rather, there were more concessions from the Morton County Sheriff's Department. In a statement, it said it would consider removing security wire and jersey barriers, in stages, *if* the camp cleanup continued and *if* protests at the bridge came to an end." She follows, "On January 20 [2017], when the Standing Rock Tribal Council voted unanimously to close the camps it was partly because of renewed clashes that erupted at the Backwater Bridge."
28. Blankenbuehler, "Cashing in on Standing Rock."
29. Ahmed, *The Cultural Politics of Emotion*, 115.
30. Ahmed, *The Cultural Politics of Emotion*, 115.
31. Rickert interview.
32. Rickert interview.
33. Collins, "Learning from the Outsider Within," 16–17.
34. Collins, "Learning from the Outsider Within," 16.
35. Collins, "Learning from the Outsider Within," 17.
36. Muñoz, *Disidentifications*, 28.
37. And that is how they differ from Muñoz's notion of disidentification, that considers the well-being of a vulnerable self who does not need to "rehearse" how power is seen from outside.
38. Anzaldúa, Gloria. *Light in the Dark*, xxxiv.
39. I mentioned in the introduction what the *elaborative* part of empathy refers to. Just to reiterate: Empathy as an elaborated emotion encompasses various sources of information that don't simply derive from emotional systems. By integrating new, incoming information from perception and memory, working memory *produces* new imaginations, *reconstructs* episodic memories, and *activates* emotional memories. These processes constitute emotional elaboration. Hogan, *What Literature*, 73–75, my emphasis.
40. Chivis, "Funeral for a Stranger," 0:54–0:59.

41. Sedgwick, *Touching Feeling*, 144.

42. Sedgwick, *Touching Feeling*, 125.

43. Sedgwick, *Touching Feeling*, 126.

44. Monet, "At Standing Rock, a Fight for Basic Survival."

45. Rickert interview.

46. Rickert interview.

47. Lingel, "Trans Literacy Project."

48. Kleinman, "Shopping in Solidarity."

49. Kleinman, "Shopping in Solidarity."

50. "Apologetical," a NPR Radiolab episode dedicated to apologies, also documented how lawyers are using the act of apologizing to significantly lower settlement dollar amounts. This episode was reported by Annie McEwen and was produced by Annie McEwen and Simon Adler. Aired on Dec 21, 2018. https://radiolab.org/episodes/radiolab-apologetical

51. Vega and Walter, "Making America Kinder," min. 45–46.

52. Monet, "At Standing Rock, a Fight for Basic Survival."

53. Smith, "Native Studies," 216.

54. From the artist' profile, www.kukulivelarde.com.

55. Here are some numbers. In little more than a century (1492–1600) Native American populations went from sixty million (ten percent of humanity's global total) to four million. Howard French, *Born in Blackness*, 124. Suketu Mehta offers equally critical numbers—in 150 years the Native population went from 100 million people to 3.5 million. Mehta, *This Land Is our Land*, 75.

56. Interview by the author with the artist, January 12–13, 2021. Hereinafter cited as Kukuli Interview. This anecdote has been shared in previous interviews. Kukuli expressed that in her second semester of graduate school at Hunter College, there was talk about celebrating the five hundredth anniversary of Columbus's arrival, and she found it offensive. She rushed to the studio and filled one of her figures with nails: "I felt for the first time that I had managed to say what I thought through my work." Roger, "Kukuli Velarde," 4.

57. Miller, "We, the Colonized Ones," 16

58. Miller, "We, the Colonized Ones," 3.

59. Miller, "We, the Colonized Ones," 3.

60. Miller, "We, the Colonized Ones," 5.

61. Miller, "We, the Colonized Ones," 9.

62. Cited in Miller, "We, the Colonized Ones," 5.

63. Miller, "We, the Colonized Ones," 8. Miller notes that the exhibition that the installation was going to be part of was banned the day before its opening in Columbus Circle. "Underdevelopment in Progress: 500 Years" was deemed "too political" by the dean at the New York Institute of Technology. See Miller, "We, the Colonized Ones," 24 n10.

64. Anzaldúa, *Light in the Dark*, 66.

65. Eeckhout and Danis, "Los tocapus reales," 305.

66. Silverman, "La tradición textil del Cusco," 98.

67. Phipps, "Cumbi to Tapestry," 95–96. We can see that the top and bottom edges of *Daddy Likee?* are bordered by lines of roses, a common feature in the tapestries from the seventeenth and eighteenth centuries that Phipps examines (79).

68. As of 2020, 64 percent of elected officials are white men, though they make only 31 percent of the American population. Rankine, *Just Us*, 21.

69. Maibom, *Empathy and Morality*, 2n1.

70. Lee, *The Beautiful*, 70.

71. Lee, *The Beautiful*, 76.

72. Lee, *The Beautiful*, 158–159.

73. Lee, *The Beautiful*, 159.

74. Lee, *The Beautiful*, 75.

75. Lee, *The Beautiful*, 75.

76. Lee, *The Beautiful*, 70; my emphasis.

77. Cited in Matravers, *Empathy*, 125.

78. Matravers, *Empathy*, 124.

79. Matravers, *Empathy*, 126.

80. Matravers, *Empathy*, 128.

81. Collingwood cited in Matravers, *Empathy*, 127.

82. I, nonetheless, found myself, recently, agreeing with Collingwood while attending two Philadelphia Orchestra concerts.

83. Smith, "Native Studies," 230.

84. Matravers, *Empathy*, 128.

85. Lopes, "An Empathic Eye," 126, cited in Matravers, *Empathy*, 130.

86. Lopes 2011 cited in Matravers, *Empathy*, 133.

87. Lee, *The Beautiful*, 163.

88. Lee, *The Beautiful*, 163.

89. Taller Puertorriqueño, "Kukuli Velarde: The Complicit Eye."

90. Taller Puertorriqueño, "Kukuli Velarde: The Complicit Eye."

91. Taller Puertorriqueño, "Kukuli Velarde: The Complicit Eye."

92. Schneider, *The Explicit Body in Performance*, 3.

93. Kukuli interview.

94. The Clay Studio, Statement Exhibition *Making Place Matter*, June 2022.

95. Kukuli interview.

96. Schneider, *The Explicit Body in Performance*, 7.

97. Kukuli interview.

98. Anzaldúa, *Light in the Dark*, 62.

99. Anzaldúa, *Light in the Dark*, 62.

100. Brackets indicate illegible text.

101. Schneider, *The Explicit Body in Performance*, 2.

102. Kukuli interview.

103. Silverman, "La tradición textil," 98.

104. Phipps, "Cumbi to Tapestry," 96, fig. 98.

105. Silverman, "La tradición textil," 105.

106. Eeckhout and Danis, "Los tocapus reales," 305.

107. Murra, cited in Eeckhout and Danis, "Los tocapus reales," 306.

108. Phipps, "Cumbi to Tapestry," 96.
109. Eeckhout and Danis, "Los tocapus reales," 306.
110. Rowe, "Standardization in Inca Tapestry Tunics," cited in Eeckhout and Danis, "Los tocapus reales," 306.
111. Christian Bendayan, personal communication, January 26, 2021.
112. Schneider, *The Explicit Body in Performance*, 2. This is painfully evident, among other current US-based examples, by the overturning of *Roe vs. Wade* that the Supreme Court made possible on June 24, 2022.
113. Brackets indicate illegible text.
114. Kukuli interview.
115. Kukuli interview.
116. Kukuli interview.
117. Altamirano, *La invención*, 134.
118. Kukuli interview.
119. Anzaldúa, *Light in the Dark*, 67.
120. Velarde website; my translation.
121. Velarde website; my translation.
122. Anzaldúa, *Light in the Dark*, 68.
123. Gilroy, *Against Race*, 114-115.
124. LaCapra, Dominick. *Understanding Others*, 45.
125. Sedgwick, *Touching Feeling*, 12–13.
126. Gilroy, *Against Race*, 115.
127. Taller Puertorriqueño, "Kukuli Velarde: The Complicit Eye."
128. Smith, "Native Studies," 221.
129. Dhillon, "Uprising 12/13," 1:15:50.

CONCLUSION

1. Smith, "Native Studies," 217.
2. Ngũgĩ wa Thiong'o, "Enactments of Power," 11–30.
3. Moraga and Anzaldúa, *This Bridge Called My Back*, xxiv.
4. See *Thousand Plateaus* by Deleuze and Guatari. In *Un apartamento en Urano*, Paul Preciado remarks, paraphrasing Deleuze and Guatari, that those are not about fleeing but about the creation of a critical exteriority with which to reopen the current of subjectivity and desire (191). Etienne Balibar in "Utopia 1/13" believes that "lines of escape" is a better translation.
5. Cherríe Moraga, Toni Cade Bambara, and Kate Rushin address these ideas around the same time that the essays collected in Spillers's *Black, White, and in Color* appeared. For example: "An Order of Constancy" appeared in 1985, "Mama's Baby, Papa's Maybe . . ." was published in 1987, and "Who Cuts the Border? Some Readings on America" was published in 1991.
6. Moraga and Anzaldúa, *This Bridge Called My Back*, xxxvii.
7. Moraga and Anzaldúa, *This Bridge Called My Back*, xxxvii.
8. Anzaldúa, *Borderlands*, 6.

9. Spillers, *Black, White, and in Color*, 323.

10. Lima, "La expresión americana." This is the first line in the essay, which is from 1957.

11. Szalita, "Some Thoughts on Empathy," 110.

12. Hogan, *What Literature*.

13. Spillers, *Black, White, and in Color*, 207.

14. Spillers, *Black, White, and in Color*, 207.

15. Calloway-Thomas, "A Call for a Pedagogy of Empathy."

REFERENCES

Ahmed, Sara. "Affective Economies." *Social Text* 79, no. 22.2 (2004): 117–39. https://doi.org/10.1215/01642472-22-2_79-117.

———. *The Cultural Politics of Emotion.* New York: Routledge, Taylor & Francis Group, 2015.

Aja, Alan A. *Miami's Forgotten Cubans: Race, Racialization, and the Miami Afro-Cuban Experience.* New York: Palgrave Macmillan, 2016.

Algarín, Miguel, and Marc Newell. *Survival = Supervivencia.* Houston, TX: Arte Público Press, 2009.

Altamirano, Carlos. *La invención de Nuestra América.* México: siglo ventiuno editores, 2021.

Althusser, Louis. "Ideology and Ideological State Apparatuses (Notes towards an Investigation)." In *Lenin and Philosophy, and Other Essays,* translated by Ben Brewster, 85–126. London: New Left Books, 1971.

Alvarado, Leticia. *Abject Performances: Aesthetic Strategies in Latino Cultural Production.* Durham, NC: Duke University Press, 2018.

———. "Ghostly Givings: Nao Bustamante's Melancholic Conjuring of Brownness." *Women & Performance: a Journal of Feminist Theory* 29, no. 3 (2019): 243–255. https://doi.org/10.1080/0740770X.2019.1671101.

Anzaldúa, Gloria. "Foreword to the Second Edition, 1983." In *This Bridge Called My Back: Writings by Radical Women of Color,* 4 ed, edited by Cherríe Moraga and Gloria Anzaldúa, 253–254. New York: State University of New York Press, 2015.

———. *Borderlands: The New Mestiza = La frontera.* 4th ed. San Francisco: Aunt Lute Books, 2012.

———. *Light in the Dark: Rewriting Identity, Spirituality, Reality = Luz en lo oscuro.* Edited by A. L. Keating. Durham, NC: Duke University Press, 2015.

Associated Press, "A Man Pleads Guilty to Federal Charges in the El Paso Shooting that Targeted Latinos." NPR, Feb. 8, 2023. https://www.npr.org/2023/02/08/1155614286/el-paso-walmart-shooting-guilty-plea-federal-hate-crime-weapons-charges.

Austin, John L. *How to Do Things with Words.* Oxford: Oxford University Press, 2009.

Báez, Josefina. "Dominicanish 1st Performance 1999." Filmed 1999. YouTube, posted September 2, 2016, video, 15:11. www.youtube.com/watch?v=OpFY7GMoWGU.

———. "Lectura y coloquio con Josefina Báez." *Conversaciones en el Observatorio.* Instituto Cervantes at Harvard University, Cambridge, MA. YouTube, posted April 16, 2014, video, 1:17:56. https://www.youtube.com/watch?v=qKO99aqS6Wo.

———. *Dominicanish.* With Photographs by Giovanni Savino. Ay Ombe Theater. Middletown, DE, 2017.

Báez, Josefina, Keyros Guillén, Carolina Sagredo, Teresa Bonilla, and Yolanny Rodríguez. *Latin in: antología de autología. Dramaturgia de Josefina Báez.* New York: Ay Ombe Theatre / I om be Press, 2013.

Balibar, Etienne. "Utopia 1/13." Center for Contemporary Critical Thought, September 28, 2022. https://blogs.law.columbia.edu/utopia1313/1–13/

Bauman, Richard. *Verbal Art as Performance.* Long Grove, IL: Waveland, 1977.

Beauvoir, Simone. *Nature of the Second Sex.* Translated and edited by H. M. Parshley. London: New English Library, 1968.

Blankenbuehler, Paige. "Cashing In on Standing Rock." *High Country News,* April 13, 2018. www.hcn.org/issues/50.6/tribal-affairs-cashing-in-on-standing-rock.

Bloom, Paul. *Against Empathy: The Case for Rational Compassion.* London: Vintage, 2018.

Bourdieu, Pierre. *The Logic of Practice.* Palo Alto, CA: Stanford University Press, 1990.

Brown, Alleen. "Five Spills, Six Months in Operation: Dakota Access Track Record Highlights Unavoidable Reality – Pipelines Leak." *The Intercept,* January 9, 2018.

Bruguera, Tania. 2013. "Dignity Has No Nationality." TED Global 2013 session, "The World on Its Head." Curated by Nassim Assefi and Gabriella Gómez-Mont. https://www.ted.com/profiles/1614089.

Bryant, B. K. "An Index of Empathy for Children and Adolescents." *Child Development* 53, no. 2 (1982): 413–25. DOI:10.2307/1128984.

Burt, Stephanie. "'She's Leaving Home': A Pioneering Trans Novel and the Trails It Blazed." *New Yorker,* June 27, 2022, 65–67.

Bustamante, N. *Indigurrito* [video], 1992. Hemispheric Institute Digital Video Library. https://hemisphericinstitute.org/en/hidvl-collections/item/1290-nao-indigurrito.html.

Butler, Judith. "Conscience Doth Make Subjects of Us All." *Yale French Studies* 88 (1995): 6–26. https://doi.org/10.1515/9781503616295-005.

Calloway-Thomas, Carolyn. *Empathy in the Global World: An Intercultural Perspective.* Thousand Oaks: SAGE, 2010.

———. "A Call for a Pedagogy of Empathy." *Communication Education* 67, no. 4 (August 2018): 495–99. https://doi.org/10.1080/03634523.2018.1504977.

Capó Crucet, Jennine. *My Time among the Whites: Notes from an Unfinished Education.* New York: Picador/St. Martin's, 2019.

Casamayor-Cisneros, Odette. "Confrontation and Occurrence: Ethical-Esthetic Expressions of Blackness in Post-Soviet Cuba." *Latin American and Caribbean Ethnic Studies* 4, no. 2 (2009): 103–35.

Cavanagh, Sarah Rose. *The Spark of Learning: Energizing the College Classroom with the Science of Emotion.* Morgantown: West Virginia University Press, 2016.

Cep, Casey. "Rescue Work." *The New Yorker*, February 3, 2020, 26–31.

Chivis, Dana. "Funeral for a Stranger." *This American Life*, National Public Radio, May 18, 2018. Audio, 18:39. www.thisamericanlife.org/646/the-secret-of-my-death/act-three-14.

Collins, Patricia Hill. "Learning from the Outsider Within: The Sociological Significance of Black Feminist Thought." *Social Problems* 33, no. 6 (Dec. 1986): s14–s32. https://doi.org/10.2307/800672.

Costello, Diarmuid, and Jonathan Vickery. *Art: Key Contemporary Thinkers.* Oxford: Berg, 2007.

"Cuba Tightens Control of Internet after Protests." *BBC News*, August 18, 2021. https://www.bbc.com/news/world-latin-america-58255554.

Currie, Gregory. "Empathy for Objects." In *Empathy: Philosophical and Psychological Perspectives*, edited by Amy Coplan and Peter Goldie, 82–95. Oxford: Oxford University Press, 2014.

de la Fuente, Alejandro. "Los afrolatinos y los estudios afrolatinoamericanos." In *Dimensiones del latinoamericanismo.* Madrid: Iberoamericana; Frankfurt: Vervuert, 2018.

Delgado, Kevin. M. "Spiritual Capital: Foreign Patronage and the Trafficking of Santería." In *Cuba in the Special Period*, edited by Ariana Hernandez-Reguant, 51–66. New York: Palgrave Macmillan, 2009. doi:10.1057/9780230618329_4.

Du Bois, W. E. B. *The Souls of Black Folk.* Chicago: A. C. McClurg; reprint, Stilwell, KS: Digireads.com, 1903.

Dukes, D., K. Abrams, R. Adolphs, M. E. Ahmed, A. Beatty, K. C. Berridge, S. Broomhall, et al. "The Rise of Affectivism." *Nature Human Behaviour* 5, no. 7 (June 10, 2021): 816–20. doi:10.1038/s41562-021-01130-8.

Durán Almarza, Liamar. "'At Home at the Border': Performing the Transcultural Body in Josefina Báez's 'Dominicanish.'" In *Transnationalism and Resistance: Experience and Experiment in Women's Writing*, edited by Adele Parker and Stephenie Young, 45–68. Amsterdam: Rodopi, 2013.

Eeckhout, Peter, and Nathalie Danis. "Los tocapus reales en Guamán Poma: ¿Una heráldica incaica?" *Boletín de Arqueología PUCP*, no. 8 (2004): 305–23. revistas.pucp.edu.pe/index.php/boletindearqueologia/article/view/2020.

Fanon, Franz. *Black Skin, White Masks.* New York: Grove, 2008.

Febvre, Lucien. *A New Kind of History and Other Essays.* New York: Harper & Row, 1975.

Felski, Rita. *Beyond Feminist Aesthetics: Feminist Literature and Social Change.* Cambridge, MA: Harvard University Press, 1989.

Foucault, Michel. 1967. "Des espaces autres (conférence au Cercle d'études architecturales, 14 mars 1967)." *Architecture, Mouvement, Continuité* 5 (October 1984): 46–49. www.foucault.info/documents/heteroTopia/foucault.heteroTopia.fr.html.

Foucault, Michel. *Power/Knowledge: Selected Interviews and Other Writings, 1972–1977*. New York: Harvester, 1980.

French, Howard W. *Born in Blackness: Africa, Africans, and the Making of the Modern World, 1471 to the Second World War*. New York: Liveright Publishing Corporation, 2021.

Frevert, U., and T. Singer. "Empathie und ihre Blockaden: Über soziale Emotionen." In *Zukunft Gehirn: Neue Erkenntnisse, Neue Herausforderungen*, edited by P. Gruss and T. Bonhoeffer, 121–46. Munich: C. H. Beck, 2011.

Fusco, Coco. *Dangerous Moves: Performance and Politics in Cuba*. London: Tate Publishing, 2015.

———. *English Is Broken Here: Notes on Cultural Fusion in the Americas*. New York: New Press, 1997.

García Peña, Lorgia. "Performing Identity, Language, and Resistance: A Study of Josefina Báez's 'Dominicanish.'" *Wadabagei: Journal of the Caribbean and Its Diaspora* 11, no. 3 (Fall 2008): 28–45.

———. *The Borders of Dominicanidad Race, Nation, and Archives of Contradiction*. Durham, NC: Duke University Press, 2016.

———. *Translating Blackness: Latinx Colonialities in Global Perspective*. Durham, NC: Duke University Press, 2022.

Gilroy, Paul. *The Black Atlantic: Modernity and Double Consciousness*. Cambridge, MA: Harvard University Press, 1993.

———. *Against Race: Imagining Political Culture beyond the Color Line*. Cambridge, MA: Belknap, 2001.

Gómez, Laura E. *Inventing Latinos*. New York: New Press, 2020.

Gonnerman, Jennifer. "The Interview." *New Yorker*, December 2, 2019, 42–53.

Guillén, Keiros. "Yo, Oy Yo." In *Latin in: Antología de autología. Dramaturgia de Josefina Báez*, by Josefina Báez, Keyros Guillén, Carolina Sagredo, Teresa Bonilla, and Yolanny Rodríguez. New York: Ay Ombe Theatre / I om be Press, 2013.

Hammond, Meghan M. *Empathy and the Psychology of Literary Modernism*. Edinburgh: Edinburgh University Press, 2014.

Harari, Yuval Noah. *Sapiens: A Brief History of Humankind*. London: Vintage Books, 2015.

"The History of Protests in Los Angeles: What Has Changed Since the Rodney King Riots." *All Things Considered*, National Public Radio, June 1, 2020. www.npr.org/2020/06/01/867256404/the-history-of-protests-in-los-angeles-what-has-changed-since-the-rodney-king-ri.

Hogan, Patrick Colm. *Affective Narratology: The Emotional Structure of Stories*. Lincoln: University of Nebraska Press, 2011.

———. *What Literature Teaches Us about Emotion*. Cambridge: Cambridge University Press, 2014.

Hogan, R. "Development of an Empathy Scale." *Journal of Consulting and Clinical Psychology* 33, no. 3 (June 1969): 307–16. https://psycnet.apa.org/doiLanding?doi=10.1037/h0027580.

hooks, bell. *Feminist Theory: From Margin to Center*. Boston: South End, 1984.

Illing, Sean. "Elites Have Captured Identity Politics." *The Gray Area* [formerly *VOX Conversations*], May 9, 2022. Podcast, 00:58:29. https://www.listennotes.com/podcasts/the-gray-area-with/elites-have-captured-IYPSmGtNua_/.

Irizarry, Roberto. "Traveling Light: Performance, Autobiography, and Immigration in Josefina Báez's Dominicanish." *Gestos* 42 (2006): 81–96.

Jolliffe, D., and Farrington, D. P. "Development and Validation of the Basic Empathy Scale." *Journal of Adolescence* 29, no. 4 (2006): 589–611. https://doi.org/10.1016/j.adolescence.2005.08.010.

"Josefina Báez, Dominican-York, Storyteller, ArteSana, Performer, Writer, Theatre Director, Educator, Joy Devotee." Website, accessed on Feb. 1, 2020. www.josefinabaez.com.

Kenya News, "Ngugi wa Thiong'o play back after 32 years," May 1, 2022. Ghanamma.com. https://www.ghanamma.com/ke/2022/05/01/ngugi-wa-thiongo-play-back-after-32-years/.

Kleinman, Avery. "Shopping in Solidarity: Can Companies Participate in Social Justice?" *The 1A*, June 9, 2020. National Public Radio, website, audio, 00:46:31. the1a.org/segments/shopping-in-solidarity-can-companies-participate-in-social-justice.

Knaller-Vlay, Bernd and Roland Ritter, eds. *Other Spaces: The Affair of the Heterotopia = die Affäre der Heterotopie.* Graz: Haus der Architektur, 1998.

LaCapra, Dominick. *Understanding Others: Peoples, Animals, Pasts.* Ithaca: Cornell University Press, 2018.

Landrove, Hilda. *A un año del 11-J* (I). *Podcast caminero.* Rialta.org, June 21, 2022. https://rialta.org/podcast-aniversario-11j-i/.

Lanzoni, Susan M. *Empathy: A History.* New Haven, CT: Yale University Press, 2018.

Lara, Ana-Maurine. "Bodies and Memories: Afro-Latina Identities in Motion." In *Women Warriors of the Afro-Latina Diaspora.* Houston, TX: Arte Público Press, 2012. http://site.ebrary.com/id/10638893.

Lee, Vernon. *The Beautiful: An Introduction to Psychological Aesthetics.* Auckland: Floating Press, [1913] 2009.

Lepore, Jill. "Data-Driven." *New Yorker*, April 3, 2023, 16–20.

Leslie, Ian. *Curious: The Desire to Know and Why Your Future Depends on It.* New York: Basic Books, 2015.

Lewis, Anthony. "Abroad at Home; A Lost Country." *New York Times*, May 3, 1992. https://www.nytimes.com/1992/05/03/opinion/abroad-at-home-a-lost-country.html.

Lima, Lázaro. *The Latino Body: Crisis Identities in American Literary and Cultural Memory.* New York: New York University Press, 2007.

Lingel, Jessa. "Trans Literacy Project Seminar on Teaching Feminist, Queer, and Trans Theory." Presentation, LGBTQ Center, University of Pennsylvania, Philadelphia, PA, October 29, 2018.

"Listen to Highlights from Acknowledgement: How Music Responds on WRTI 90.1." *Jazz with Bob Perkins.* June 2, 2020. WRTI.org, www.wrti.org/post/listen-highlights-acknowledgement-how-music-responds-wrti-901.

Lomas, Laura. "The Unbreakable Voice in a Minor Language: Following José Martí's Migratory Routes." In *Hispanic Caribbean Literature of Migration: Narratives of Displacement*, edited by Vanessa Pérez Rosario, 23–38. New York: Palgrave Macmillan, 2010. doi:10.1057/9780230107892_2.

Maibom, Heidi L. *Empathy and Morality*. New York: Oxford University Press, 2014.

Maillo-Pozo, Sharina. "Home Is WHERE Theatre Is: Aproximación al método creativo de Josefina Báez." *Revista de teatro latinoamericano, Casa de las Américas*, no. 184 (July–September 2017): 66–72. http://www.casadelasamericas.org/publicaciones/revistaconjunto/184/revista.html.

"Many Haitians Leave Dominican Republic after Court Decision," NPR, Morning Edition, Nov. 28, 2013. https://www.npr.org/2013/11/28/247635908/many-haitians-leave-dominican-republic-after-court-decision.

Martí, José. "Nuestra América." *La Revista Ilustrada de Nueva York*, January 10. Reprinted in *El Partido Liberal* (Mexico), January 30, 1891. Available at ciudadseva.com/texto/nuestra-america.

Martínez, Ernesto Javier. *On Making Sense: Queer Race Narratives of Intelligibility*. Palo Alto, CA: Stanford University Press, 2013.

Matravers, Derek. *Empathy*. Cambridge: Polity Books, 2017.

May, Charlie. "A State Ravaged by Oil: 745 Oil Spills Reported in North Dakota in Just One Year." *Salon*, May 7, 2017. www.salon.com/2017/05/07/a-state-ravaged-by-oil-north-dakota-has-reported-745-oil-spills-in-just-one-year/.

McGarry, Kevin. "The New Muse | Nao Bustamante." *T Magazine*, June 19, 2009. https://tmagazine.blogs.nytimes.com/2009/06/19/the-new-muse-nao-bustamante.

Mehta, Suketu. *This Land Is Our Land: an Immigrant's Manifesto*. New York: Farrar, Straus and Giroux, 2019.

Miller, Ivor. "We, the Colonized Ones: Peruvian Artist Kukuli Speaks about Her Art and Experience." *American Indian Culture and Research Journal* 20, no. 1 (1996): 1–25. https://doi.org/10.17953/aicr.20.1.b756081542q301vj.

Monet, Jenni. "At Standing Rock, a Fight for Basic Survival." *Indian Country Media Network*, Jan. 31, 2017. https://web.archive.org/web/20170914150211/https://indiancountrymedianetwork.com/author/jenni-monet/.

Moraga, Cherríe, and Gloria Anzaldúa, eds. *This Bridge Called My Back*, 4th ed. New York: State University of New York Press, 2015.

"Multado con 3.000 pesos un activista cubano por sus publicaciones en Facebook." *Diario de Cuba*, April 23, 2020. diariodecuba.com/derechos-humanos/1587655598_17316.html.

Muñoz, José Esteban. *Disidentifications: Queers of Color and the Performance of Politics*. Minneapolis: University of Minnesota Press, 1999.

———. "Feeling Brown: Ethnicity and Affect in Ricardo Bracho's 'The Sweetest Hangover (and Other STDs).'" *Theatre Journal* 52, no. 1 (2000): 67–79. doi:10.1353/tj.2000.0020.

———. "Stages: Queers, Punks, and the Utopian Performative." In *Cruising Utopia: The Then and There of Queer Futurity*, edited by José Esteban Muñoz,

97–113. New York: New York University Press, 2009. https://doi.org/10.18574/nyu/9781479868780.003.0011.

———. "The Brown Commons: The Sense of Wildness." *JNT Dialogue 2013: José Muñoz and Samuel Delany* (Part 1/4). YouTube, April 1, 2013, video, 00:34:56. www.youtube.com/watch?v=F-YInUlXg04.

———. "Fragment from the Sense of Brown Manuscript." *GLQ: A Journal of Lesbian and Gay Studies* 24, no. 4 (October 2018): 395–97. https://doi.org/10.1215/10642684-6957730.

Ngũgĩ wa Thiong'o. "Enactments of Power: The Politics of Performance Space." *TDR* 41, no. 3 (Autumn 1997): 11–30. https://doi.org/10.2307/1146606.

Pêcheux, Michel. *Language, Semantics and Ideology*. London: Palgrave Macmillan, 1982.

Pérez Firmat, Gustavo. *Life on the Hyphen: The Cuban-American Way*, revised ed., Austin: University of Texas Press, 2012. muse.jhu.edu/book/18200.

Phelan, Peggy. *Unmarked*. London: Routledge, 1993.

———. "Performance, Live Culture and Things of the Heart" In conversation with Marquard Smith. *Journal of Visual Culture* 2, no. 3 (Winter 2003): 291–302. https://doi.org/10.1177/147041290300200300.

Phipps, Elena. "Cumbi to Tapestry: Collections, Innovation, and Transformation of the Colonial Andean Tapestry Tradition." In *The Colonial Andes: Tapestries and Silverwork, 1530–1830*, edited by Elena Phipps, Johanna Hecht, Cristina Esteras Martín, and Luisa Elena Alcalá. New York: Metropolitan Museum of Art, 2004. https://libmma.contentdm.oclc.org/digital/collection/p15324coll10/id/121641.

Pidorych, Frank Ajete. Glosas al nuevo Código Penal cubano. *El Estornudo*, June 3, 2022. https://revistaelestornudo.com/codigo-penal-cubano/.

Piper, Adrian. "Cornered." Video art installation. In the collection of the Museum of Contemporary Art Chicago, 1988.

Plamper, Jan. *The History of Emotions: An Introduction*. Oxford: Oxford University Press, 2017.

Pocock, J. G. A. *Pensamiento político e historia: ensayos sobre teoría y método*. Madrid: Ediciones Akal, 2011.

Preciado, Paul B. *Manifesto contrasexual*. Barcelona Editorial Anagrama, 2011.

———. *Un apartamento en Urano: Crónicas del cruce*. Barcelona: Anagrama, 2019.

Propst, Andy. "Josefina Baez' *Dominicanish* Part of Harlem Stage's Fall Season," TheaterMania, August 10, 2009. *New York City.* theatermania.com.

Ramírez, M. A. *Nuestra América: Chicanos y latinos en Estados Unidos (una reinterpretación sociohistórica)*. México: Universidad Nacional Autónoma de México, 2008.

Rankine, Claudia. *Just Us: An American Conversation*. London: Penguin Books, 2021.

Reddy, William. "Historical Research on the Self and Emotions." *Emotion Review* 1, no. 4 (2009): 302–15. https://doi.org/10.1177/1754073909338306.

———. *The Navigation of Feeling: A Framework for the History of Emotions*. Cambridge: Cambridge University Press, 2010.

"El régimen echa mano a otro decreto-ley para acallar las denuncias en tiempos de Covid-19." *Diario de Cuba*, April 22, 2020. diariodecuba.com/derechos-humanos/1587586651_17197.html.

Reuters. "Former Atlanta Officer Charged in Brooks Killing Surrenders to Authorities." *Reuters*, June 18, 2020. https://www.reuters.com/article/us-minneapolis-police-atlanta-idUSKBN23P2UI.

Rivera, Alex. "Alex Rivera Speaking at Platform Summit 2014." YouTube, November 19, 2014. Video, 18:13. www.youtube.com/watch?v=eHPsmfLdiUs.

Rivers, Nathaniel. "Apathy." In *A New Handbook of Rhetoric: Inverting the Classical Vocabulary*, edited by Michele Kennerly. University Park: Pennsylvania State University Press, 2021.

Roger, Miriam. "Kukuli Velarde: La cultura precolombina desde la ironía." *ESTEKA*, no. 10 (2011).

Rossi, Enzo, and Olúfẹ́mi Táíwò. "What's New about Woke Racial Capitalism (and What Isn't): 'Wokewashing' and the Limits of Representation." *Spectre* (2020) https://philarchive.org/rec/ROSWNA-2.

Rushin, Kate. "The Bridge Poem." In *This Bridge Called My Back*, 4th ed., edited by Gloria Anzaldúa and Cherrie Moraga, xxxiii–iv. New York: State University of New York Press, 2015.

sarahfuller12345. "Adrian Piper 'Cornered.'" *GCOP200* (blog), February 6, 2014. sarahfullergcop200.wordpress.com/2014/02/06/adrian-piper-cornered.

Sawin, Patricia E. "Performance at the Nexus of Gender, Power, and Desire: Reconsidering Bauman's Verbal Art from the Perspective of Gendered Subjectivity as Performance." *Journal of American Folklore* 115, no. 455 (January 2002): 28–61. https://doi.org/10.2307/542078.

Scheer, Monique. "Topographies of Emotion." In *Emotional Lexicons: Continuity and Change in the Vocabulary of Feeling, 1700–2000*, by Ute Frevert et al., 32–61. Oxford: Oxford University Press, 2014. https://doi.org/10.1093/acprof:oso/9780199655731.003.0002.

Schneider, Rebecca. *The Explicit Body in Performance*. London: Routledge, 1997.

Sedgwick, Eve Kosofsky. *Touching Feeling: Affect, Pedagogy, Performativity*. Durham, NC: Duke University Press, 2003.

Sherry, Michael. "Home Fires." *New Yorker*, May 8, 2023, 74–78.

Silverman, Gail P. "La tradición textil del Cusco y su relación con los tocapus Incas." *Tupac Yawri: Revista Andina de Estudios Tradicionales* 1 (2008): 97–107.

Smith, Andrea. "Native Studies at the Horizon of Death: Theorizing Ethnographic Entrapment and Settler Self-Reflexivity." In *Theorizing Native Studies*, edited by Audra Simpson, 207–34. Durham, NC: Duke University Press, 2014. https://doi.org/10.1515/9780822376613-010.

Spillers, Hortense. *Black, White, and in Color: Essays on American Literature and Culture*. Chicago: University of Chicago Press, 2003.

Stearns, Peter, and Carol Stearns. "Emotionology: Clarifying the History of Emotions and Emotional Standards." *American Historical Review* 90, no. 4 (1985): 813–36. https://doi.org/10.1086/ahr/90.4.813.

Stevens, Camila. *Aquí y Allá. Transnational Dominican Theater*. University of Pittsburgh Press, 2019.

Szalita, Alberta B. "Some Thoughts on Empathy: The Eighteenth Annual Frieda Fromm-Reichmann Memorial Lecture." *Contemporary Psychoanalysis* 37, no. 1 (2001): 95–111. https://doi.org/10.1080/00107530.2001.10747069.

Taller Puertorriqueño. "Kukuli Velarde: The Complicit Eye." Press release, 2018. https://tallerpr.org/the-complicit-eye.

Táíwò, Olúfẹ́mi O. 2022. *Elite Capture: How the Powerful Took over Identity Politics (and Everything Else)*. Chicago: Haymarket Books, 2022.

———. "Elites Have Captured Identity Politics." *The Gray Area* [formerly *VOX Conversations*], May 9, 2022. Podcast, 00:58:29. https://www.listennotes.com/podcasts/the-gray-area-with/elites-have-captured-IYPSmGtNua_/.

Torra, Alex, dir. *¡Bienvenidos Blancos! or Welcome White People!* Performance at the Philadelphia Fringe Festival 2018. vimeo.com/271729083.

———, dir. *¡Bienvenidos Blancos! or Welcome White People!* 2020 Performance at Swarthmore College, Swarthmore, Pennsylvania. vimeo.com/429286213/09d4b8b1cc.

Torres-Saillant, Silvio. "The Tribulations of Blackness: Stages in Dominican Racial Identity." *Latin American Perspectives* 25, no. 3 (1998): 126–46. https://doi.org/10.1177/0094582X980250030.

Torres-Saillant, Silvio, Ramona Hernández, and Blas R. Jiménez. *Desde la orilla: hacia una nacionalidad sin desalojo.* Santo Domingo, DR: Ediciones Manatí, 2004.

"Uprising 12/13: Standing Ground." Columbia University, Center for Contemporary Critical Thought, June 14, 2018. Panelists: Dhillon, Jaskiran, Julian Brave NoiseCat, Leanne Simpson, and Nicole Willis. YouTube, video, 2:27:43. www.youtube.com/watch?v=Rnyq2UzctQE.

Van Gelder, Sarah. "Why I Knelt before Standing Rock Elders and Asked for Forgiveness." *Yes! Magazine*, December 21, 2016. https://www.yesmagazine.org/democracy/2016/12/21/why-i-kneeled-before-standing-rock-elders-and-asked-for-forgiveness.

Velarde, Kukuli. *We the Colonized Ones.* Ceramics exhibit. 1992.

———. *Daddy Likee?* 2018. Exhibit, Pennsylvania Academy of Fine Arts, Philadelphia, Pennsylvania.

———. *A mi Vida.* June 2022. Ceramics collection display and performance piece, The Clay Studio, Philadelphia, Pennsylvania.

———. n.d. *Plunder Me Baby.* Ceramics exhibit. www.kukulivelarde.com/site/Ceramic_Work/Pages/PLUNDER_ME_BABY.html.

———. n.d. Reviews of Exhibits. kukulivelarde.com/site/Reviews.html.

Vega, Tanzina, and Amy Walter. "Making America Kinder, One Smile at a Time." *The Takeaway*, December 25, 2018. Audio, 00:48:06. www.scpr.org/programs/the-takeaway/2018/12/25/67349/.

"Wesley Clark Jr. Apologizes to the Lakota Nation." YouTube, uploaded by Vineyard Saker, December 6, 2016. Video, 00:02:45. www.youtube.com/watch?v=FWU1NBcElSQ.

"What Does White Allyship Look Like at This Moment?" *The Takeaway.* National Public Radio podcast, June 2, 2020. www.wnycstudios.org/podcasts/takeaway/segments/what-does-white-allyship-look-moment.

Wilkerson, Isabel. *Caste: The Origins of Our Discontents.* New York: Random House, 2020.

Willis, Nicole, Dhillon, Jaskiran, Julian Brave NoiseCat and Leanne Simpson. "Uprising 12/13: Standing Ground." Columbia University, Center for Contemporary Critical Thought, June 14, 2018. YouTube, video, 02:27:43. www.youtube.com/watch?v=Rnyq2UzctQE.

Wittgenstein, Ludwig. *Philosophical Investigations.* New York: MacMillan, 1958.

Zelizer, Julián. "30 Issues, a History of Criminal Justice and Policing," *Brian Lehrer Show*, National Public Radio, July 13, 2016. www.wnyc.org/story/30-issues-history-criminal-justice-and-policing.

Printed in the USA
CPSIA information can be obtained
at www.ICGtesting.com
CBHW021946230824
13639CB00004B/101

9 780826 506733